THE DUAL VOICE

THE DUAL VOICE

Free indirect speech and its functioning in the
nineteenth-century European novel

Roy Pascal
Litt.D., F.B.A.

Manchester University Press

Rowman and Littlefield

Published by
Manchester University Press
Oxford Road
Manchester M13 9PL

ISBN 0 7190 0654 6

Published in the United States 1977 by
Rowman and Littlefield
Totowa, New Jersey 07512

ISBN 0 87471 927 5

Typeset at the Minor Press
Printed and bound in Great Britain at The Pitman Press, Bath

Contents

Preface

> Gwendolen's dominant regret was that after all she had only nine louis to
> add to the four in her purse; these Jew dealers were so unscrupulous in
> taking advantage of Christians unfortunate at play!

The stylistic device that this study investigates occurs in one of its
simplest forms in the above passage from George Eliot's *Daniel
Deronda*. It will be observed that the second, exclamatory sentence,
though grammatically identical with the first, cannot like the first be
an authorial statement—since it asserts an opinion the novel sets out
to show is a prejudice—but must express a view held by the character,
Gwendolen.

While working on the style of a German writer, Arno Holz, I came
across several examples of this stylistic form, but was surprised to find
it was not commented on in critical analyses of this author's prose. I
vaguely recognised it to be something the Germans call 'erlebte Rede',
but had no clear idea of what this is, so I began to enquire into it, discussing it with friends and in lectures. I found that to most people it
was little and vaguely known, but with the help of a few published
studies I was able to track down the first identification and analysis of
the device, its first name 'le style indirect libre', and the arguments
that led the Germans to invent their substitute for this term, 'erlebte
Rede'.

In the course of numerous discussions I found that scholars in
French studies are more familiar than others with this stylistic form,
and have in Professor S. Ullmann's *Style in the French Novel* (1957) a
convenient and reliable account of its functioning in French literature.
Two further recent studies in French are *Etude de grammaire
historique et de style sur le style direct et les styles indirects en
français* (Groningen, 1959), by J. A. Verschoor, and 'De l'origine du
prétendu "style indirect libre" ', by A. Kalik-Teljatnicova, in *Le
Français Moderne,* XXXIII and XXXIV, 1965 and 1966. All German
scholars know the term 'erlebte Rede', though few could define it accurately, and amongst those who can there is much doubt about its
suitability. The definitions of the form and accounts of the history of

its theoretical identification given in Werner Hoffmeister's *Studien zur erlebten Rede bei Thomas Mann und Robert Musil* (1965) and Dorrit Cohn's article, 'Narrated monologue. Definition of a fictional style' (*Comparative Literature* (Oregon), XVIII, 1966), though informative and critical, leave much unexplained and uncertain. English literary scholars have traditionally been less responsive to the grammatical aspects of stylistics, and as late as 1958 Professor Randolph Quirk could say, in *Charles Dickens and Appropriate Language,* that English has 'no generally acknowledged term' for this device. Such studies of its incidence in English literature as have been published till recently have all, I believe, been by German or Swiss scholars (Dorrit Cohn gives a bibliography). Interest has quickened in the past few years. Many scholars are now familiar with the term 'free indirect speech', some having doubts as to its suitability. Perceptive if brief comments on its use in George Eliot's *Middlemarch* are to be found in Derek Oldfield's contribution to *Middlemarch: Critical Approaches to the Novel,* ed. Barbara Hardy (1967), and its functioning in *Emma* has been skilfully delineated in Graham Hough's essay, 'Narration and dialogue in Jane Austen' (*The Critical Quarterly,* XII, 1970). Professor N. Page has discussed the use of the form by Jane Austen in chapter 4 of *The Language of Jane Austen* (1972), and has also given a precise account of the form in general in his *Speech in the English Novel* (1973), though the account is very brief and examples are taken from only two or three novels. Some of the linguistic and grammatical problems involved have been discussed by P. Guiraud in 'Modern linguistics looks at rhetoric: free indirect style' (in *Patterns of Literary Style,* ed. J. Strelka, 1971), and by A. Banfield in 'Narrative style and the grammar of direct and indirect speech' (*Foundations of Language,* X, 1973). There are probably other contributions that I have overlooked.

I originally intended to write a short essay on this topic, to go with a group of stylistic studies of German prose in which free indirect speech occurs. But the material and problems swelled, and the interest that the subject aroused in discussion encouraged me to write a longer study. I came to think that, instead of making a systematic, abstract analysis, it would be more fruitful to describe the arguments of the first essays on this stylistic form, for the old controversy both provides the material for a critical definition and allows us to judge of the relative merits of the designations 'style indirect libre' and 'erlebte Rede'. Since its various functions can only be examined in the actual texts, Part 2 of this investigation is devoted to practical criticism.

Only nineteenth-century texts have been chosen, and this historical limitation was decided on so that it would be possible to show in what ways this device was first widely used, and how its scope extended up to that moment when its potential resources were uncovered. For that reason I have led up to, but not discussed, Henry James, and have contented myself with a few occasional references to later masters—and elaborators—of the style like James Joyce, Virginia Woolf, and William Faulkner. In commenting on its occurrence I have also been concerned with its absence; so I have tried to define the conditions under which it can appear and thrive, the type of narrative it can serve, the sort of fictional environment in which the need for it makes itself felt. Such matters are most complex, as indeed is the analysis of the functioning of the device in a given context; many of my observations no doubt require elaboration and modification. But I wished to keep this study short, and should not mind disagreement provided interest is aroused.

I wish to thank many friends in the University of Birmingham for sympathy, criticism, and suggestions, especially Professor Terence Spencer and Mrs Katharine Spencer, Mrs Elsie Duncan-Jones, and David Lodge; also Professor R. Hinton Thomas and the members of the German Department of Warwick University, and Professor H. B. Nisbet and the German Department of the University of St Andrews, for inviting me to lecture and take part in discussions. And above all I wish to thank my wife for her interest, her tolerance of innumerable conversations on this topic, and especially for the help she has given me with Russian texts.

PART 1

Theory

The narrator problem

Novelists have always sought to present the inner life, the mental and emotional activities and responses of their invented characters, and for this purpose have used direct and indirect means: the direct are the actual words a character uses in speech or writing, the indirect include the description of events and behaviour, of the environment a character constructs around him, as well as the descriptive account of what he said, thought, and felt. The limits of what can be revealed through conversation and letters, even if stretched to the brink of credibility, are soon reached, since it must remain within the bounds of what a character knows and can formulate, and also of what may properly be communicated to another person. Various other devices have therefore been invented to extend the range of a fictional character's direct utterance, notably the self-communing reflection, the soliloquy, a transference of an ancient theatrical device to the novel. For many decades, in fact, the epic monologue took the form of actual speech, often prefaced by an introductory phrase like 'he thought to himself', and enclosed, like normal direct speech, in inverted commas. We find such speech-monologues throughout the nineteenth century, and not rarely in the twentieth. William Faulkner uses them extensively in *Light in August*, sometimes (though not systematically) indicating different levels of consciousness by using italics for some parts of this thought-speech. They occur abundantly in J.-P. Sartre's *Les Chemins de la liberté*, usually in a patchwork with indirect speech and narratorial description.

The enrichment of insight thus gained is however tainted. That such formalised self-communing is not true to life is in itself not a disqualification; the soliloquy has its indubitable right in certain types of drama. But, in the novel, extensive verbalisation of this nature invites a psychological interpretation, and may seem to imply a high degree of rationalising self-consciousness in the character which may, in many cases, conflict with his or her temperament or situation. Further, such soliloquies may easily acquire a rhetorical tone, such as is inappropriate to private musings, and this because it is hard for formal prose to shake off its life-function as communication to others, that is, the presupposition of a listener. It thus may involuntarily take on the accent of argument or persuasion, when it might be intended to be a spontaneous reaction or a pure search for inner clarification. If one were in life to speak to oneself as Stendhal's Fabrice or Fontane's Innstetten do, one would properly be suspected of wily, conscious or unconscious scheming.

From the dawn of the genre, the first-person novel has provided a solution to some part of this problem, since the narrator can describe out of self-knowledge, from the vantage-point of his latter life, all the psychic constituents of his self-hero in the past. But this freedom in regard to the fictional self entails a larger limitation in regard to other characters than hampers an impersonal third-person narrator, who is allowed the right of access to all secret places. Where the first-person narrator is not a chief character, but only a bystander, he suffers of course still greater handicaps. There are other difficulties arising from the form of the first-person novel, which have frequently led authors palpably to strain its capacity. Henry James, when contemplating its advantages and disadvantages in the Preface to *The Ambassadors,* admits that it might have permitted him to 'smuggle in' certain sorts of formally illicit items, but expresses his unease over the 'freedom' taken by the authors of *Gil Blas* and *David Copperfield,* where the hero is both subject and object of the story. He concludes that one could adopt this form 'only if one is prepared not to make certain precious discriminations'—these for James would be connected with consistence of narrative perspective and a delicate appreciation of the degree of self-consciousness pertaining to each character. We can see examples of what James wished to avoid in the first-person sections of *Bleak House,* for on several occasions 'Esther's Narrative' contradicts Esther's character as Dickens intended it to appear merely by the fact that she is over-selfconscious, and as a result priggish and self-admiring. The same sorts of difficulty arise in the epistolary novel.

All these narrative forms suffer also from another limitation that might, indeed, be considered a fundamental presupposition of story-telling altogether. That is, the narrator is removed in time from the events described, so that these are recounted from the perspective of their outcome, and through the medium of a narrator whose present temperament, situation, and style must be very different from those of the persons engaged in the story. The epistolary novel was a means to overcome this double distance, but did so only by forfeiting other rights. In more modern times, the consciousness of the transforming,

3

perhaps distorting power of distance has led to the invention of a narrative that keeps as close as possible to the events as they occur, like that of Arthur Schnitzler's first-person, present-tense novels *Leutnant Gustl* (1901) and *Fräulein Else* (1924). In these there is no time-gap—or only the smallest—between the event and the record, so that, lacking the perspective of retrospection, the stories capture the indeterminacy that belongs to living. There are two serious drawbacks to this form. The insistent self-awareness of the narrators can be appropriate at a brief climax of anguish or terror, but cannot be maintained over longer and less tense periods without suggesting a neurotic condition (Schnitzler wisely made these stories short). But the other drawback is more troublesome. The verbalisation involved in this form, the continual transformation of situation and action into words, is in the Schnitzler stories intended simply to evoke the troubled and confused awareness of the character. In fact, it retains the quality of speech as communication, as information conveyed to another person or to the reader, and there is something very disturbing in this insistence on telling us what is going on. Something is achieved, the unconscious self-revelation of Gustl's baseness or of the neurotic pressures in Fräulein Else, but at times the narrative borders on the absurd. Of course, this form also creates great technical difficulties, and it creaks at the joints when other people than the narrator–hero are described.

In the sketch *Der Apostel* (1890) Gerhart Hauptmann made an interesting attempt to fuse this direct reproduction of a character's experience with the authorial, third-person mode. The sole function of the non-personal narrator is to adopt the perspective of the apostle, a religious enthusiast; the man himself, his thoughts, the environment through which he moves, appear only as he himself sees them and knows them. The use of third-person, authorial narrative excludes the excessive self-consciousness that may cling to the extended inner monologue, and the sketch is a brilliant and disciplined piece of narrative prose. It lacks any other perspective, visual or moral, than that of the character. Since the work is very short—Hauptmann called it 'a study'—this is no handicap, but in a longer work this lack might become both cramping and wearisome. Still, one might see in this sketch an anticipation of Kafka's form, in which the narrator is almost completely confined to the perspective of the hero; and it is no accident that in Kafka's three novels, as in Hauptmann's sketch, the absence of an independent, authorial point of view, balancing the hero's, contributes to the feeling of a neurotic obsession that the novels give us.

It is not with these structural devices that we are here concerned, but with a stylistic device, or form, that arose from the general search for means to present the inner life of the characters of a novel. This is the 'style indirect libre', first named and identified by the Swiss linguist Charles Bally in 1912. The discovery of the functioning of this form occurred in the years when writers and critics first found theoretical formulations of the structural principle of narrative perspective, and though the identification of the two groups of problems remained separate, they are clearly associated as belonging to the modern development of the novel as well as of novel-theory. Before embarking on an account of Bally's discovery, I believe it is helpful to give a sketch of the much-discussed emergence of the theory of narrative perspective.

The latter third of the nineteenth century was preoccupied, as far as novel-theory was concerned, mainly with an ideal of 'objective' narration. More and more attacks were delivered against the traditional obtrusive author of the type to be found in Thackeray's *Vanity Fair*, who in his own person continually intervenes in his story to explain and make moral comments, to interpret his work to his readers. Through the novels and theory of Flaubert and the Realist or Naturalist schools, in Germany through the effective critical essays of the novelist Friedrich Spielhagen, the idea gained wide acceptance that the author's presence must be obliterated, that he must speak only through the creations of his imagination, the events and characters of his story. But no sooner was this theory accepted than lively arguments arose over a concept of objectivity that meant, as for Zola, that the novel was comparable with a scientific experiment and the author with a scientist, or that the author must reduce himself to a recording eye, a camera. How, if so, was a fictional story to be constructed? Where begin and where end it? And it was Henry James, in the prefaces he wrote for the New York edition of his complete works, who most pertinaciously and fruitfully proposed answers to these questions.[1]

James shared the distaste of Flaubert and Spielhagen for the obtrusive author and what he called 'the muffled majesty of irresponsible authorship' to be found in Balzac and Dickens. But his answer was not the demise of the narrator, but the concept of the 'point of view', of narrative perspective. What he requires of a novel is that the 'feel of life' of the fictional characters should be created, the feel of the choices open to them; a moral evaluation, if it is to be genuine and valid, can emerge only from the possibilities of *their* world, *their* personality, *their* mode of experience. These objectives can be achieved only if the reader can get 'within the skin' of the characters, can see and understand in their terms, from their perspective, without of course sacrificing his own objective position. No more, then, of the Olympian author who delivers judgements from outside the story. But James, in one sense diminishing the presence and powers of the author, in another, like Flaubert, greatly increases his responsibilities, in that those easy, armchair judgements of a Thackeray now are replaced by a much more scrupulous and firmer-founded discrimination. He does not lessen the responsibility of the author but embeds it within his creation.

A German dissertation of 1910 by Käte Friedemann was, I believe, the first systematic defence of the narrator as the essential structural principle of the novel; it does not seem in any way to be indebted to Henry James.[2] Taking up the cudgels against Spielhagen and the Naturalists, with their theoretical objective of presenting reality 'without a medium'—a theory which, as she rightly says, could not possibly be realised—Käte Friedemann claims that 'the most self-evident reality' of a story is the fact that it is told by a narrator to an audience; and by the very story-situation, distance is established between the events narrated and the teller (and listener or reader). She goes on to analyse the various ways in which stories are devised, the first and decisive condition being, in her view, the choice of a 'Blickpunkt', an angle of vision. Käte Friedemann was a pupil of Oskar Walzel, certainly one of the least blinkered academic literary critics of that time, but his published comments on her book show some embarrassment. For while he admires her 'most weighty' defence of what he calls descriptive narrative, as opposed to the scenic–dramatic trend of the novels of Spielhagen and the Naturalists, Walzel accepts the latter as the dominant and modern form. Little did he know what had been brewing in Dublin.[3]

Käte Friedemann's dissertation was little known or considered, and it was left to Percy Lubbock, in *The Craft of Fiction* (1921), to systematise Henry James's observations and to make the 'centre of vision' a familiar term and an acknowledged principle of narrative structure. According to this principle, there are three models of the novel as Lubbock defines them: that with an external, 'omniscient' narrator; that with a first-person narrator; and a third, in which the narrator works and appears only through the medium of his story and of the consciousness of his characters. Lubbock's terminology is not very satisfactory, particularly as he does not clearly differentiate between

6

'author' and 'narrator'. In a recent German study, F. K. Stanzel suggests the terms 'authorial novel' for the first type, and 'personal novel' for the third.[4] But these too are not satisfactory, since 'authorial' does not distinguish between the person who writes—Henry James or George Eliot—and the supposed narrator, who is often not a person at all and enjoys the privileges of a disembodied intelligence that has access to the secrets of heart and mind and can be ubiquitous. 'Personal novel' is distinctive enough in German, but ambiguous in English. A formal terminology is however required, and in what follows I shall use 'author' for the real, historical person who writes, and 'narrator' for the teller of the tale, whether personal or non-personal; the adjectival form 'narratorial' is clumsy, but seems indispensable. In some contexts the distinction is superfluous, and in some situations cannot clearly be drawn. For 'personal' in Stanzel's sense, 'subjective' may be used, in distinction to the 'objective' and authoritative nature of a narratorial description or statement, or some descriptive phrase that indicates that a statement or description represents the words, thoughts, vision of a character.

Among the illuminating themes in Lubbock's study, one of the most relevant to this present investigation is his awareness of the double role of the narrator. Lubbock makes it clear that, while he greatly admires Henry James's obliteration of the narrator behind his characters (for instance, behind Strether in *The Ambassadors*), he also reckons it to be a great gain that at times the narrator 'edges away' from the character, delicately claiming a separate identity. The narrator, says Lubbock, may become invisible if he is not 'a value in himself', but he is often such, and as such has a function in the story. Lubbock therefore recommends 'the old familiar mixed method' of novel-writing, in which the author finds it advantageous to change the perspective from time to time.

None of these early investigators of the principle of narrative perspective speaks analytically of associated stylistic or grammatical forms. Käte Friedemann, when discussing the Naturalist author Arno Holz, does seem to be theoretically aware of the narrator's power to describe through the medium of his characters' consciousness, but dismisses it as producing too complex and confusing an effect. Lubbock defines in chapter 17 of *The Craft of Fiction* the narrative situation in which a fusion of narrator and character occurs, but does not describe or analyse the syntactical form this fusion takes. In the course of the controversy that arose over Bally's concept of 'style indirect libre', however, the relationship of this device to the problem of narrative perspective was soon observed.

7

II

'Le style indirect libre'

Free indirect speech was first described and analysed in 1912 by Charles Bally, then a lecturer at the University of Geneva, and a former pupil of F. de Saussure. He was not the first to observe it. An article of 1897 by A. Tobler had drawn attention to a 'peculiar mixture' of direct and indirect speech and had tried to account for the blending of indirect forms of person and tense into what otherwise seemed to be direct speech. T. Kalepky discussed Tobler's article in 1899, but came to the conclusion that this mixture was a literary device to pass off authorial opinions through the medium of fictional characters. A Swedish dissertation of 1905 by Elis Herdin discussed examples of this stylistic phenomenon that he found in German fiction from the eighteenth century to his own day, but this very useful piece of research remained practically unknown and without effect. Bally was the first to recognise it to be an independent and significant stylistic form and to give it a distinctive name. His article, 'Le style indirect libre', appeared in the most enterprising academic periodical of the time, *Germanisch–Romanische Monatsschrift* (*GRM*), which linked critics and philologists in French, English, and German, and it there kindled a lively controversy from which a whole type of stylistic studies has grown.[5]

When reporting the discussion of Bally's term (literally 'free indirect style'), I will use the abbreviation SIL. After the English equivalent 'free indirect speech' has been adopted, FIS will replace SIL.

Bally defines three possibilities of rendering the words or thoughts of a character, the first two being long known to grammarians. My example is slightly more elaborate than his:

1. *oratio recta* (direct speech): He stopped and said to himself, 'Is that the car I saw here yesterday?'

2. *oratio obliqua* (indirect speech): He stopped and asked himself if that was the car he had seen there the day before.

3. an unrecognised form (SIL): He stopped. Was that the car he had seen here yesterday?

This third type has the syntactical form of a normal authorial report, as we find it in simple indirect speech, and the second part of it is grammatically identical with No. 2. That is, in place of the first person and the present tense of direct speech, both the other forms have the third person and the past tense ('he' for 'I', 'was' for 'is'). But the second part of No. 3 is clearly not a question posed by the author to a reader; it is directed by the character 'he' to himself. In our example, the deictic adverbs 'here' and 'yesterday' both clearly inform us that the question asked reflects the situation, in time and place, of the character, and hence must emanate from the character, not the author. The curious thing about No. 3 is that this form uses the character-reference of direct speech—'here' and 'yesterday'—though normal indirect speech, No. 2, requires 'there' and 'the day before', indications appropriate to an informant speaking about another person.

The simplest description of No. 3 would be that the narrator, though preserving the authorial mode throughout and evading the 'dramatic' form of speech or dialogue, yet places himself, when reporting the words or thoughts of a character, directly into the experiential field of the character, and adopts the latter's perspective in regard to both time and place.

The sequence of tenses in our example is a very common one. But of course, the introductory verb 'stopped' might be in the present or the future tense. The tense of reported, indirect speech is determined by that of the introductory verb, and thus would be present if 'stops' were used instead of 'stopped'; if the introductory verb were in the future, then the conditional would be required in indirect speech. Even in our example we cannot carry out simple replacements of this kind, and further problems arise in more complicated statements than this. With some of these we shall be concerned later. The example given provides us with a reasonably satisfactory basis for the examination of Bally's theory and its critics.

Since this third form has the pronouns and tenses of simple indirect speech, Bally considered its name should indicate this relationship. Further, since in distinction from simple indirect speech it has no linking conjunctions ('that', 'whether', etc.), and may often lack the introductory verb, *verbum dicendi* or *credendi* ('he said', 'he thought', etc.), Bally associated the term 'free' with 'indirect'. He noted, however, that the form has some of the distinctive features of direct speech, and gives the feeling of direct speech. While simple indirect speech tends to obliterate the characteristic personal idiom of the reported speaker, SIL preserves some of its elements—the sentence form, questions and exclamations, intonation, and the personal vocabulary—just as it preserves the subjective perspective of the character. Bally recognised therefore that it is a curious mixture of indirect and direct speech, but believed that its syntax indicated that it was more correctly to be associated with indirect than direct speech. Indeed, he thought its origin might have been, in a normal account, in indirect form, of the words or thoughts of a person, the simple elimination of the wearisome repetition of verbal introductions like 'he said', 'he thought', and of repeated conjunctions—'he said that . . ., that . . ., and that . . .' etc. It must however be considered a terminological weakness that 'style indirect libre' in itself bears no reference to the presence of expressive elements from direct speech.

Bally acknowledged that SIL cannot be defined solely in grammatical terms. On grammatical grounds it often cannot be distinguished from normal authorial report, and as a result pointers like 'he thought' may be required to make it clear that a statement emanates from the character and not from the author. Frequently the reader cannot, in fact, be sure whether a statement belongs to one or the other. SIL is also, syntactically, a very loose form. While as a rule the tense-system is similar to that of simple indirect speech (e.g. in a narrative told in the past tense, statements that in direct speech would be in the present or the future are, in indirect speech, in the past or conditional), the many examples that Bally proffers show a remarkable variety in the sequence of tenses, so that he concludes that the form 'enjoys an almost absolute syntactical liberty'. He also notes that it can almost bewilderingly alternate in a patchwork with other forms, with direct speech, simple indirect speech, and authorial narrative, and he observes in La Fontaine's verse, as in Flaubert's prose, 'a veritable to-and-fro' of the different forms. However, it is often not difficult to detect, owing to the frequent presence of stylistic indicators, 'indices' as Bally calls them. In his first article he mentions some of these only in a note—exclamations like 'alas', oaths like 'my God', appellations like 'Madame', and a large number of particles that in certain contexts bear a subjective reference and indicate an argument going on within the character's mind—'so', 'thus', 'doubtless', 'besides' ('donc', 'ainsi', 'sans doute', 'd'ailleurs') among others. The types of indices are more thoroughly analysed in Bally's second article of 1914.

Bally's conclusion is that SIL is not a distinctive grammatical form but a stylistic one. Indeed, he shows that it sometimes may play havoc with conventional grammar and syntax. For instance, the tense adopted for the SIL statement may 'contaminate' by 'attraction' verbs outside the statement, or 'grammatical monstrosities' may occur that nevertheless are stylistically effective and logical. This may be one of the reasons why Bally calls the form a 'style', 'free indirect style', rather than 'speech', 'discours'. But it is probable that he used the third term of his designation, 'style', without much reflection, since, though *oratio recta* and *obliqua* are often, in French, called 'discours direct' and 'indirect', they are as often called 'style direct' and 'indirect', and these are the terms Bally himself uses. The Germans, who, like the English, translate *oratio* by 'speech' ('Rede'), are naturally inclined to use this same term when looking for an equivalent for 'style indirect libre'.

Though in his first article Bally quotes striking examples of SIL from La Fontaine, he recognises that before the nineteenth century this stylistic device occurs only spasmodically and incidentally; it is only in the last hundred years, he writes (in 1912), that it has become a distinctive feature of prose-writing, reaching full stature in Flaubert and Zola. His analysis is devoted entirely to French usage, and it was some time before scholars came to realise how widespread the device is in the modern European languages.

In both articles, of 1912 and 1914, Bally discusses at some length a feature peculiar to French that he discovered was a signal of 'style indirect libre'. This is the use of the past imperfect tense (the 'imparfait') for SIL statements that occur in the framework of a narrative told in the preterite. It was already known to linguists at that time that the use of the 'imparfait' in place of the preterite in normal narrative statements may heighten the listener's or reader's sympathetic self-identification with the subject of the verb concerned, and Bally's observation was in part indebted to this. But when he called this tense a 'subjective imperfect' he also meant that it is not a true past but has a past form only because it is governed by the tense of the surrounding narrative. An example that Bally adduces, that was much discussed in the ensuing controversy, shows both the typical use of this 'imparfait' within SIL, and the contagious effect it may have on the narrative tense (*loc. cit.*, p. 552). It is taken from the beginning of Prosper Merimée's *Colomba,* when the Colonel is putting to Lydia the arguments against her journey to Corsica:

> In vain he spoke about the wildness of the country and the difficulty for a woman to travel through it: she was afraid of nothing; she loved travelling on horseback above everything; it was a treat to sleep in the open air; she threatened to go to Asia Minor.

En vain il parla de la sauvagerie du pays et de la difficulté pour une femme d'y voyager: elle ne craignait rien; elle aimait par-dessus tout à voyager à cheval; elle se faisait une fête de coucher au bivac; elle menaçait d'aller en Asie Mineure.

The 'style indirect libre' is signalled in the French text by the change from preterite 'parla' to imperfect 'craignait', 'aimait', 'se faisait', 'menaçait', a change which cannot be reproduced in English, though in English too the content makes clear that the last sentences all give Lydia's answers. But why the imperfect for 'menaçait'? The preceding SIL statements can be taken as reproducing Lydia's direct speech: 'I fear nothing', 'I love travelling on horseback', 'It's the greatest treat to sleep in the open air'. But we do not imagine her saying, 'I threaten to go to Asia Minor'; all she would say would be something like 'I shall go to Asia Minor'. That is, the 'threaten' is the narrator's interpreta-tion of what she said, and is functionally no different from 'he spoke' at the beginning. Why, then, is it not in the preterite? Bally came to the conclusion that the imperfect here is the result of the 'attraction' of the imperfect in the preceding SIL statements, and he found examples of the same sort of contamination in other texts. Though other scholars were reluctant to accept his analysis, it still seems the most persuasive. To put it in a slightly different way: while the imperfect tense earlier is a 'subjective past', and does not refer to any event in the true past, the threat is an event in the story, part of the historical sequence.

German provides Bally with a vexatious problem, for, as he knew, it has a form of indirect speech, sometimes called 'festgestellte Rede' ('reported speech'), that does not need conjunctions, and may even dis-pense with an introductory *verbum dicendi,* but which signals itself as reported speech through the use of the subjunctive—'er sagte, er sei heute beschäftigt'. English too has an indirect form without conjunc-tions, though it normally lacks the signal of the subjunctive—'he said he was busy today'. Thus Bally was aware that the 'free' in his designation 'style indirect libre' could not distinguish the SIL form in German and English from other indirect forms, for 'free' was intended to mean 'free of conjunctions'. In his first article, indeed, he seems to think SIL does not exist except in French, and satisfies himself, in regard to German, with an attempt to prove that SIL is the French equivalent for the German indirect with the subjunctive, claiming that both introduce the same quality of directness into indirect speech. He translates a passage from Schiller in this form into French, using 'style indirect libre', to prove it. His example is not persuasive, since in the German the narrator is much more obtrusive than in the French. E. Lorck, who was later to point out Bally's mistake in equating the two forms, was also to observe that the German 'festgestellte Rede' can never shake off the implication that it is reporting actual speech or print, rather than thoughts.

In the last part of his first article Bally briefly considers the possible sources of literary SIL. He comes to the conclusion that it does not occur in common linguistic usage and is purely a product of writing. He therefore calls it not a figure of speech but a 'figure of thought' ('figure de pensée'), which he defines as 'a type of thought characterised by a conflict between the thing thought and the linguistic signs by which it is expressed'.

In the following year Bally's theses provoked a severe reproof from the Berlin professor T. Kalepky, a philologist and literary scholar of prestige.[6] Kalepky refers to his earlier dispute with Tobler over the phenomenon that Bally had analysed, and again maintains that it is not a true form of indirect speech. He corrects Bally by showing that his form may be used in German as well as French, but asserts that German has, in the indirect form with the subjunctive, a clearer and more convenient form of reported speech. However, while rejecting Bally's interpretation of SIL, Kalepky does admit it has a function in French. His own interpretation starts from the observation that certain exclamations and oaths may have, in SIL, the form of 'Just think!' or 'My God!', and these demonstrate that the third person is not always characteristic of SIL statements. Such exclamations Kalepky takes to be unguarded outbursts of the writer, that betray the true nature of SIL as a masked expression of authorial opinion, smuggled in in this form in order to ingratiate itself with the innocent reader. Similarly, Merimée's use of the imperfect in 'menaçait', discussed above, is a momentary fumble of the writer's sleight of hand. Kalepky uses passages from Zola to drive home his argument. In place of Bally's designation he finally proposes that the form should be called 'Verschleierte Rede' ('veiled speech') or 'Verkappte Rede' ('disguised speech').

Kalepky's interpretation arises from only peripheral aspects of the style, and most of his conclusions are inept. But, though the suggestion that the form is a mere trick of an author is absurd, there was some truth in his argument that Zola does sometimes manipulate SIL in order to smuggle in his own views. There was also some justification for his dissatisfaction with the term 'style indirect libre'. In the

13

following year, 1914, two German scholars, both working in French studies, were to respond more positively and with sounder criticism to Bally's initiative.

In an article on the French past definitite, past indefinite, and imperfect tenses, Etienne Lorck refers to Bally's article only briefly.[7] Respectful as he shows himself to Kalepky, he recognises the full validity of the stylistic form Bally has described, in German as well as in French. He argues in Bally's sense that it directly communicates the experience of the fictional character, in spite of its authorial, indirect form. In a significant phrase he claims that it demonstrates that the writer, in such passages, 'inwardly experiences' the thought and feeling of the character concerned, and in these words, 'innerlich miterlebe', we can see the germ of the German equivalent for SIL, 'erlebte Rede' (literally 'experienced speech'), that Lorck was later to invent.

But Lorck also criticises Bally. In some forms and contexts, he writes, SIL makes an effect closer to that of direct speech than indirect, so that it is misleading to label it 'indirect'. He considers that the reason for its being rarer in German than in French is that German lacks a distinctive past-imperfect tense, which in French often serves to identify 'style indirect libre'. Finally Lorck agrees with Bally that SIL cannot be found in common usage, and he suggests that it can occur in literature only because an author, in the act of writing, can be alone with his imagined characters in the seclusion of his study, and only in this privacy—which the presence of a second person shatters—can immerse himself into the psyche of his imaginary creatures.

Later in the same year, in the same periodical, another contribution dealt a still more crushing blow to those who either doubted the identity of Bally's form in general or questioned its legitimacy in German. This was an essay with the somewhat forbidding title 'The stylistic significance of the imperfect of speech (style indirect libre)', by Eugen Lerch, a lecturer at Munich. This little-known study is a modest landmark in stylistics, since it was the first to analyse the use of 'style indirect libre' in the context of the whole structure of a work, and this work a German novel, Thomas Mann's *Buddenbrooks* (1901).[8] From this moment, refusal to acknowledge the existence and unique function of SIL could only be excused by ignorance.

In one respect Lerch continues the criticism of Bally's terminology. He insists, like Lorck, that the reader feels that SIL passages are near to direct speech in their substance, though their syntax places them nearer to indirect speech. The distinctive effect of SIL, he holds, is the authorial authority it gives to what is, in fact, only the view or thought of a character. In the title of his article he suggests a new name for the form, 'the imperfect tense of speech', but in the course of his argument suggests another possibility, 'speech as fact' ('Rede als Tatsache'). To these we shall return in the section on 'Erlebte Rede'.

Lerch goes on to a practical demonstration of SIL through a study of *Buddenbrooks*, a work of high literary quality, the style of which could not be dismissed as incorrect or vulgar. He makes a number of grammatical observations, notably on the curious moods as well as tenses to be found in SIL, so that for instance what appears in direct speech as a subjunctive may appear in SIL in the indicative. But the importance of the essay lies in the field of literary criticism. It investigates the various ways in which SIL works, why it is used in certain contexts and situations, or for certain characters: for instance, what effect it produces when a conversation, or some parts of it, is narrated in SIL, while other parts may be in direct speech; or why the exaggerated and melodramatic speech of Makler Gosch is often given in the medium of SIL. In his analyses Lerch shows in what ways such passages bear the imprint of the character, and vividly evoke his presence, for instance through intonation or characteristic personal vocabulary, while at the same time Lerch shows that they exercise narratorial functions, convey the narrator's valuations, notably his irony. The skilful and perceptive stylistic analysis is linked with that of the narrative structure. Demonstrating that the narrative focus of the novel is the Buddenbrook family, and that events or scenes are described only from the angle of vision of one or more of the Buddenbrooks, Lerch shows that SIL is thus an integral expression of the narrative process. If the narrator, to describe a room, a landscape, a character, adopts the focus of the family for his normal narratorial style, it is natural and functional that he should, on many occasions, identify himself still closer with the family through SIL. Its tone and distribution are also determined by the over-all perspective, and it is used in a very limited way for characters on the periphery of the family (just as the discarded husbands Grünlich, Permaneder, and Weinschenk all disappear from the book once they drop out of the family).

Lerch considers SIL in a still wider context. Building on Bally's sketch of its historical incidence and its efflorescence in the nineteenth century, Lerch links it with the formal development of the European novel altogether, suggesting that it is a significant agent and symptom

15

of the general trend of the novel away from the discursive, descriptive, authorial novel of event and action towards the modern dramatic or scenic, psychological type.

Here, however, Lerch fails to integrate the new insights gained from the recognition of 'style indirect libre' with those on narrative perspective that we associate with Henry James. In line with the popular theoretical trend that Käte Friedemann had tried to refute, Lerch writes that the modern novel has become more 'dramatic', by which he means that story is replaced by dramatic scene, that 'the author completely withdraws'. It is the slogan 'exit author' that we have so often heard since that time; by 'author' is meant narrator.[9] Lerch then claims that SIL is a notable instrument in this process of dramatisation, since we see events, when described in 'style indirect libre', through the field of experience of the characters, without the intervention of a narrator. Now, it is true that the narrator in *Buddenbrooks* is not obtrusively present. But this does not mean that he is not there, with an angle of vision of his own and also his own moral evaluation. Lerch himself, though his conclusion seems to deny this, had shown that many passages in SIL bear an ironical tone. Whose irony? Lerch does not ask, but it is clear that while in some instances the irony may belong to one of the characters, in many it is so subtle and sophisticated that it is beyond the mental scope of any Buddenbrook. Thus, the ironical treatment of Makler Gosch may in part reflect Thomas Buddenbrook's attitude towards him, but it is also far too imaginative and exuberant for the reserved Hamburg senator. So also the ironical tang in the reflections of the family doctor, Grabow, which are presented in SIL, is alien to the family and in places beyond the doctor himself (part I, chapter 7). The SIL form of Tony's acceptance of Grünlich, upon her father's urging, sparkles with the narrator's irony which, on this important matter, no Buddenbrook would share with him (part III, chapter 3). On all such occasions, the narrator is moulding and guiding the reader's response.

We can at times clearly detect in Lerch's analyses the misleading influence of his general thesis. When Thomas tries to sidestep his sister Tony's plea for a divorce, we read (part VI, chapter 11):

> He had no time. He was, by God, overwhelmed with business. She should be patient and be so kind as to think it over another fifty times!

> Er hatte keine Zeit. Er war bei Gott überhäuft. Sie sollte sich gedulden und sich gefälligst noch fünfzigmal besinnen!

Lerch makes the comment that this piece of SIL not only gives us the intonation, haste, irritation with which Thomas speaks, but also guarantees the truth of what he says. But this is not so. It is true we vividly feel the nervous strain in Thomas's words, but the passage in no sense attests that he really had no time. Explicitly we hear that he has no time; but the irritation in each of his phrases, intensified by the concentrated form and arrangement of the three sentences, makes us suspect he is finding excuses for his reluctance. There is, therefore, irony in this passage, a rectification of Thomas's viewpoint through the counterpoise of the author's ironic criticism. The duality of narrator and character is still felt in 'style indirect libre', and may be heard as a tone of irony, or sympathy, of negation or approval, underlying the statement of the character. Lerch fails to formulate this double function of SIL, to hear it as a 'dual voice'. We shall see that his inclination to overstress the expressive, subjective function was to be embodied in the German term for SIL, 'erlebte Rede'.

In between these two articles by Lorck and Lerch was sandwiched Bally's reply to Kalepky, 'Figures of thought and linguistic forms'.[10] Here Bally provides a fuller and more systematic analysis of 'style indirect libre'. He first enumerates the 'external indices' of the form, i.e. the authorial material that introduces or qualifies the passage in SIL, and then the 'internal indices'. The latter include the interplay of objective narrative and SIL, and that between direct speech, simple indirect speech, and SIL; syntactical indicators like tenses and persons (pronouns); others like particles, appellations, exclamations, and characteristic personal idiom, all of which point to the subjective source of the statement. He enlarges the scope of SIL beyond the reproduction of words and thoughts to include the inarticulate vision of the characters, their sentient and nervous response to the outer world, the description, for instance, of the countryside through their eyes. This latter comment is made in respect of Zola's usage. A further observation may have been due to Kalepky's accusation that SIL is authorial sleight of hand. For Bally now states that no one has 'used and abused' SIL more than Zola, and that in the late novels, *Rome* and *Lourdes*, he seeks to impose his own ideas through the ostensible ruminations of his heroes.[11] Generally, Bally had no difficulty in showing Kalepky's criticism to be inept.

In the course of this article Bally quotes from many more modern French authors and detects a great variety of function in the form. He finds a number of SIL or near-SIL passages in Rousseau's *Emile* too. More importantly, he discovers SIL in a modern German author, though Lerch's article on *Buddenbrooks* was soon to confirm its existence in German much more substantially. In his first article Bally had quoted examples of its use in French historical and biographical writing, and now he quotes with relish an example from an English critical article published in the same periodical (*GRM*). But he never, I believe, discusses the effect and appropriateness of 'style indirect libre' in non-fictional prose, just as he never discusses what type of novel promotes its use.

Bally's chief concern in this second article of 1914 is the relationship between SIL and common usage, what he calls 'life', and he maintains his earlier opinion that it is not prefigured in actual speech but is a product of literature, of sophisticated literature. Since this question is of no great importance for my purpose in this study, I may at this point sum up the course of the ensuing controversy over it.

Bally himself quotes some examples of SIL from literary texts that sound suspiciously like ordinary conversational usage, and in the article by Lerch quoted above there are some examples of SIL drawn from common parlance—such as the remark one might make after visiting a hypochondriac: 'Oh, he's at the point of death again', a phrase compounded of mimicry and irony. But Lerch draws no conclusion from this observation. Lorck, in his article, had emphatically supported Bally on this issue. So far as I know, the first critic to challenge this aspect of Bally's theory was A. Thibaudet, in other respects a grateful debtor. In his *Gustave Flaubert* of 1922 Thibaudet follows Bally in discerning Flaubert's varied and subtle use of 'style indirect libre'.[12] But he emphatically claims that the form is indeed common in ordinary speech. He gives an example: a sergeant will ask his officer for leave on behalf of a private in his platoon in some such terms as: 'He's asking to go on leave; his sister is making her first communion.' The second phrase clearly quotes the private's application and, as Thibaudet says, the tone in which it is spoken will also communicate the sergeant's opinion of its genuineness. Incidentally, Thibaudet insisted that, of all the subjective elements in statements in the SIL form, the intonation was the most constant and characteristic. But in his comment on the sergeant's voice he is suggesting that SIL bears a double intonation, that of the character and that of the narrator, that it is, in fact, a dual voice.

Later in the decade Thibaudet's view was more and more widely supported. Leo Spitzer, another Romance scholar, gave it solid backing in 1928, claiming that the simplest definition of SIL (by now he uses the German term, 'erlebte Rede') is mimicry, and that mimicry implies a mimic as well as a person mimicked. Later in that year Lerch stated that it was now generally accepted that the origin of the form was to be found in common usage.[13] He believed that there occur in common speech more complex forms of 'erlebte Rede' than even Thibaudet allowed for.

Not everyone agreed with these linguists. Oskar Walzel, in his theoretically rather superficial accounts of 'erlebte Rede', still sticks to Bally's view,[14] as does Marguerite Lips, Bally's pupil, in her *Le Style indirect libre* of 1926. It would seem, however, that Thibaudet and Spitzer were right; the study of certain texts later in this book, notably of Jane Austen, will give an opportunity of judging. But Lerch certainly seems to underestimate the distance between the forms found in common parlance and in literature. Thibaudet's formulation seems the most satisfactory, for while he claims that ordinary speech is its source, he also says that common usage only gives the first impetus, and what the writers do is to follow this up, 'load up with its electrical charge'. He rightly points out that it needed writers of great artistry to adopt and establish this stylistic device and thus to give to literary, non-spoken language 'the sensation of the spoken language'.[15] In this complexity the 'style indirect libre' is typical of literary style that recovers the simple expressiveness of speech only by means of the most subtle devices. These it needs if only to restore to the printed page the auditory and gestic quality of actual speech in a form that can fill the imagination of the solitary reader.

To return to the further clarification of the concept of 'style indirect libre':

The outbreak of war put an end to the lively controversy of 1912–14, but the main features of SIL were now agreed on, and in Germany the chief concern was the clarification of the psychological functioning of the device and the invention of an appropriate German name. Etienne Lorck's *Die 'erlebte Rede'* of 1921 renewed the discussion, and provided German scholars with their terminological equivalent, which was, with some misgivings, rapidly adopted. With this book, and the term, we shall be concerned in the following section. Thibaudet's intelligent analysis of SIL in Flaubert's novels (1922) did much to establish the value of Bally's work for the literary critic. In Germany, Walzel's essays, referred to above, not only popularised the concept among students of literature but also contributed the information that 'erlebte Rede' could be found in the older German novel as well as the modern, in Wieland and in Goethe's *Werther, Wilhelm Meister's Apprenticeship,* and *The Elective*

Affinities. One further document claims our attention, a dissertation, *Le Style indirect libre* (1926) by Marguerite Lips. This excellent systematic investigation is essentially based on French literature, but it includes a brief review of SIL in the German and English novel.[16]

Dr Lips' study, itself firmly based on Bally's teaching, gives an outline of the controversy that arose out of his first article on SIL. It extends Bally's contributions in respect of both formal analysis and stylistic interpretation, and may have been influenced by the stress on the expressive aspect of SIL by Lerch and Lorck. Dr Lips examines the expressive features in many examples, and formulates it clearly: 'It [SIL] allows the retention of the exclamations, intonations and in general the expressive features proper to direct speech; the syntax of propositions is independent, no introductory transitive verb; free indirect speech (like simple indirect) transposes the tenses and the personal pronouns'.

Dr Lips demonstrates systematically the functioning of the 'indices' and other accompaniments of SIL, ejaculations and oaths, particles and verbs with a subjective reference, rhetorical questions etc. She rightly points out that the question form in which SIL statements are frequently cast scarcely ever indicates a true question that awaits an answer, but is rhetorical, exclamatory. It is odd that she, like Bally, does not seem to recognise one of the most striking signals of SIL, the combination of the past tense of simple indirect speech with such deictic adverbs as 'now', 'tomorrow', 'next Tuesday', 'here' etc, which normally can be used only with the present or future tense. It was, in fact, the recognition of the association of these deictic adverbs with an apparently contradictory verbal tense that was much later to set Käte Hamburger off on her investigation of the nature of the preterite used in fiction and her theory of fictional time.[17]

Dr Lips is less concerned with grammar than Bally, and more with style. Thus she is attentive, when examining Flaubert, to occasions when SIL is not used, as well as when it is. She develops Bally's suggestion that SIL can reproduce not only the words and thoughts of a character but also his visual perspective, and shows how descriptions of persons, places, rooms, etc. are sometimes governed by the perspective of a character, sometimes not (she may have profited here from Lerch's study of *Buddenbrooks* as well as Thibaudet's *Flaubert*). She gives a brief outline of the incidence of SIL in French literature, filling out Bally's sketch, and she is, so far as I know, the first critic to recognise its frequent presence in Jane Austen's novels and to admire the great skill with which Jane Austen handles it (she chiefly examines passages from *Sense and Sensibility*). She mentions its occurrence in Russian literature and the difficulty that the Russian tense-sequence causes the analyst.

This admirable study, which combines delicacy of perception, precision of interpretation, and theoretical clarity, may be considered to close the period of discovery of free indirect speech. It still leaves a number of questions either unresolved or faultily formulated. What processes take place in the reader when he reads a passage of SIL, or a page in which it alternates with other forms? In what way, in what order, does he apprehend the double presence of character and narrator? Is it accurate to say that he momentarily slips into the skin of a character? How does his response vary from that to direct speech and simple indirect speech? Is the idiom of SIL statements identical with that of the direct speech of the character concerned? What inherent linguistic resistances are there to the transference of certain figures of speech in direct speech and narratorial report into the free indirect style? And what semantic modifications occur when such transferences are made? Are there conditions that prevent or discourage the use of SIL? What type of narrator does it require? What is the effect of its use in historical, biographical, and critical writing?

These and other questions can only be answered by the examination of texts. But before we turn to them, we need to know how the Germans came to adopt their term for SIL, 'erlebte Rede', whether it means the same, and which is the better. We might also ask, why has this form scarcely been recognised by English scholars, and why is it still little known and little understood? But this question is a sleeping dog we'll let lie.

III

'Erlebte Rede'

We have already seen that German scholars who acknowledged the identity and distinctive function of 'le style indirect libre' still did not think Bally's analysis or his terminology satisfactory. 'Freedom', i.e. freedom from conjunctions, did not distinguish it from other forms of indirect speech in German and English; and 'indirect' failed to do justice to the direct evocation of the speech and tone of a character through the use of SIL. Bally would not have disputed this criticism, so far as it goes.

But, even in their first response to Bally's article, Lorck and Lerch proceeded from this point to make the direct evocation of the character the distinctive feature of 'style indirect libre'. Lorck wrote that it arose in a state of intense imagination, when the writer so identifies himself with the creatures of his imagination that he 'inwardly experiences' what they experience. Lerch maintained that in SIL passages the narrator disappears from the scene to be replaced by the character, whose self-expression borrows the narratorial form only in order to assume the full authoritativeness of narratorial statements ('Rede als Tatsache'—'speech as fact').

This pre-war controversy was recalled in 1921 by Etienne Lorck in his little book, *Die 'Erlebte Rede'*. This is the work that established the term 'erlebte Rede' in German stylistics; its nearest and literal equivalent in English would be 'experienced speech'.

Lorck's argumentation and interpretation were not primarily empirical. They belong to his whole conception of language. He was a member of Karl Vossler's school, the investigations of which were, as he proudly defined them, 'research into the soul of language' ('Sprachseelenforschung'); the term might be explained as investigation into the psychological processes from which linguistic forms spring and which they stimulate. All Lorck's observations on 'erlebte Rede' are purposefully related to this general linguistic approach. When he criticises Bally for being too much the prisoner of grammar, he is expressing the principle of the Vossler school that one must penetrate to the spirit behind grammar, a principle that encouraged much valuable enquiry but also some far-fetched speculation. His search for a psychological definition of Bally's phenomenon, to replace the purely grammatical definition that Bally's term formulates, belongs to an adherent of Vossler.

The chief empirical observation in Lorck's theory is that, in SIL statements, we hear direct speech, not reported speech, and in his sense experience directly what the character is experiencing, through the medium of the character's own words. Oddly enough, he does not differentiate it from the use of direct speech, and in his book he illustrates his interpretation of the psychological process in the listener or hearer by an example from Goethe's *Faust,* i.e. from the direct speech of a dramatic character. When the audience hears Faust's opening monologue: 'I've now, alas! studied philosophy, law, and medicine, and unhappily theology too', according to Lorck it 'experiences' it in the third person: 'Faust has now, alas! studied philosophy, law, and medicine, and unhappily theology too, etc.' That is, the hearer thinks of Faust in the third person but understands him in the character's own terms, his own ejaculations and intonation, as Faust understands himself. SIL is the literary form that records, in narrative form, this psychological process of identification of audience and character in the theatre.

To this odd piece of psychological analysis Lorck adds a still more questionable one on the creative process in the writer, repeating at great length what he had claimed in his 1914 article. SIL occurs, he writes, at those heightened moments of creativity when the writer's imagination transports him into his characters, when he surrenders to their existence and falls into a state of 'utter raptness' ('völliges Entrücktsein'), oblivious of his real environment and the world. It was in the first place to this notion that the concept 'erlebte Rede' owed its birth, and this seems to be the dominant meaning Lorck gives it in his book. Passages of 'erlebte Rede' arise therefore at moments of high poetic frenzy, and are different in character from other parts of the narrative, in which the contriving artistic reason dominates. When we pursue Lorck's argumentation further, we discover that this distinction is less empirical (indeed it could not be maintained on empirical grounds) than theoretical, for we find it arises from a general assertion that there are two sorts of language, the imaginative and the rational, and two uses of language, one to communicate experience and the other to communicate information. 'Erlebte Rede' was thus especially dear to Lorck, since it was an example, a proof, of the imaginative type and the irrational function of language.

Bally was therefore wrong, Lorck concludes, to call his form a variety of indirect speech. He admits that it is a link between direct speech and objective narrative, even in some sense a fusion of the two, but it is 'direct speech immediately experienced' ('unmittelbar erlebte direkte Rede')—again we note the failure to discriminate between direct speech and SIL. Lorck taunts Bally with having first overlooked the existence of SIL in German, and claims that the fact that it is found in German proves that 'it could not possibly have had its origin' in simple indirect speech. Lorck does not further substantiate this rash claim; did he base it on the fact that simple indirect speech in German requires the 'subordinate' order, in which the finite verb is transferred to the end of the clause, while free indirect speech enjoys the normal order? But why does 'erlebte Rede' have in other respects the syntactical forms of indirect speech, why in particular is, in a narrative, the present tense of direct speech transformed into the past tense? Because, Lorck argues, the 'erlebte Rede' passages relate to a real past in the memory of the writer, who is writing down an (imaginary) 'auditory experience' ('Gehörerlebnis') he had had. Bally had insisted that the tenses of SIL statements are determined by the tense of the introductory verb, i.e. of the narrative, and that they should not be confused with true temporal statements; Lorck dismisses Bally's concept of the 'subjective past tense' and claims that the tense of a SIL passage indicates a real time.

Lorck's contention is, to say the least, frail, but it does attract attention to a problem that Bally did not discuss. If, within SIL statements, a generalisation is made, a general truth or proverb is enunciated—such as 'necessity knows no law'—this may be left in the present tense, even though the introductory verbs and other verbs within the SIL are in the past tense. This distinction, Lorck argues, is due to the fact that these generalisations embody a universal, timeless truth, while the past tense of the SIL statement indicates an event in time. However, Lorck overlooks the fact that generalisations may also be put in the past tense in the SIL form—'necessity knew no law'—just as a 'timeless' question, 'What is death?' can appear, in the SIL passages in which Thomas Buddenbrook is suddenly confronted by this question, as 'What was death?' From such cases one might triumphantly argue that Bally was right in denying the past tense of SIL any true temporal meaning. In fact, since we find that both the present and the past can be used for such generalisations, we have to look further for an explanation (the problem is discussed below, pp. 49, 83, 96, 101, and Notes 28 and 29, in relation to examples from Walter Scott, George Eliot, Trollope, and Flaubert). It may be said at this point, however, that while Lorck's theory that the past tense in 'erlebte Rede' refers to a past 'auditory experience' of the writer is odd to the point of ecentricity, we do discover that, on occasion, some temporal meaning attaches to the past tense of SIL passages, usually through some contextual influence.

On several occasions Lorck refers to the supporting opinion of Lerch, especially as arising from the latter's analysis of *Buddenbrooks*. But he does not approve of Lerch's term and concept of 'speech as fact' ('Rede als Tatsache'). While Lerch claims (see above pp. 14–17) that SIL clothes the character's view in the authority of a narratorial guarantee, Lorck more sensibly insists on the purely subjective testimony of statements in this form; that is, their function and value lie entirely in the sphere of subjective experience, not objective truth. In 1928 Lerch was still obstinately to maintain that he was right in this and that Lorck ought logically to have adopted his view.

The great importance of 'erlebte Rede' for Lorck, and the chief reason he invented this term, arose from his belief that it embodied the irrational function of language, communicating experience, not objective information. It is ultimately the same reason that led him to support Bally's contention that SIL has no counterpart in normal linguistic usage and is purely literary in origin; for, if as Lorck says, it arises in the exteme privacy of the imagination and is frustrated when two or three are gathered together, he means that it belongs to a type of language that is absent from normal social intercourse.

With Lorck's theory of language we cannot deal here. All that is to be judged is the accuracy of his stylistic observations, and this can be tested only by the examination of texts that the Part II of this study undertakes. But the results of this examination can be anticipated.

In his theory, as in his analysis of texts, Lorck fails to recognise the narratorial function of the 'style indirect libre'. Almost all critics and linguists, among them Stephen Ullmann and Norman Page, have recognised that it fuses the narratorial and the subjective modes.[18] Lorck uses a similar phrase, but in fact ignores everything apart from the subjective function, the direct evocation of the character, the contrast to simple indirect speech and to normal narratorial description. But SIL always embodies a narratorial element, clearly proclaimed in the first place through the verbal tense and the pronominal forms.

The narratorial presence is communicated in three main ways: through the vocabulary and idiom; through the composition of the sentences and longer passages; and through the context.

Usually Lorck sees the 'erlebte Rede' passage as embodying the actual (imagined) words of a character. Only once in his analyses does he recognise that a narratorial word, indicating a narratorial interpretation, is embedded in an 'erlebte Rede' passage (from *Buddenbrooks,* describing Hanno's terror at school of being called on to translate). Lorck offers a complicated explanation, but calls it an 'exceptional case' ('Sonderfall'). But it is not. The idiom of SIL passages varies greatly, from being close to the narrator's own style, e.g. in Goethe's *The Elective Affinities,* to being a close mimicry of a character's idiom, e.g. in Zola. Always the language is mixed, implying an interpreting intermediary; often of course it bears a strong implicit narratorial comment, notably of irony. Most critics have pointed out the ironic function of SIL in Goethe, Jane Austen, Thomas Mann and others.

The narrator also makes himself felt through the form and order of the sentences. 'Erlebte Rede' is different from direct speech in that it does not claim to report speech literally; it is, or always may be, a résumé, a condensation, an ordering of what goes on in the mind of the character, or of what he said, with a view to distinguishing the main features, the main purport, of his thought or utterance. This ordering of the (imagined) raw material clearly serves the purpose of the narrator, whether this be a moral or psychological comment or the articulation of the material into a narrative, i.e. into a structural context. These two aspects are normally combined, of course, and are brilliantly illustrated in the SIL passages evoking Dr Grabow and Makler Gosch in Thomas Mann's *Buddenbrooks.* Neither Lerch nor Lorck, who both admire these passages, notices that the language and the composition are not solely subjectively determined, but reveal the imagination and the irony of the narrator.

It is pre-eminently for these reasons that we hear in 'style indirect libre' a dual voice, which, through vocabulary, sentence structure, and intonation subtly fuses the two voices of the character and the narrator.

Lastly, the presence of the narrator in 'erlebte Rede' passages is insinuated through the syntactic context, through the interweaving of the free indirect form with the narratorial mode and with direct speech. Lorck himself observes that its introduction into a narrative requires some bridge—for instance the neighbourhood of direct or simple indirect speech, or an introductory verb such as 'he stopped', 'he was frightened'—through which attention is directed at the experiencing character. But this must mean that, instead of our experiencing the SIL statement, as Lorck claims, as something qualitatively different from other forms of discourse, we normally experience it within a broader consciousness that implies distance between characters and the narrator (and reader). Actually, a passage in SIL may be introduced with the very slightest bridging mechanism, so slight indeed that only the content may indicate to which character it attaches. Such sophisticated handling of the device, common in the twentieth century but not infrequent in the nineteenth, was not noticed by Lorck, but it only reinforces doubts on the validity of his subjective interpretation of the style.

These empirical characteristics of the 'style indirect libre' force us, as I believe, to repudiate the major rectifications that Lorck proposed to Bally's interpretation of the style. But the term 'erlebte Rede' owed its birth and its justification precisely to Lorck's supposed rectifications; and, as I have indicated, to a general theory of language which must almost seem eccentric. In English, then, we are well advised to reject the German term, together with the general theory implicit within it, and stick to something nearer Bally's terminology; we are thus, incidentally, fortunately spared the hopeless task of finding a translation for 'erlebte Rede'.

How was it that the Germans accepted it? Contemporary reviews of Lorck's book in Germany contain a number of criticisms of his theory and analysis, but show a general inclination to accept his term 'erlebte Rede' as the most apt designation of what was felt to be the dominant trait of this stylistic device, namely, the direct communication of the character's experience. We can confine our attention to the views of Oskar Walzel, an authoritative scholar, the first Germanist of note to affirm the identity and importance of 'erlebte Rede'. It was above all through his agency that the concept became widely accepted among literary scholars, and he stimulated many stylistic investigations. His fullest account of the device was given in an article of 1924, and this was reprinted in his book, *Das Wortkunstwerk,* of 1926; an abbreviated form of it in *Gehalt und Gestalt* (1924) holds some rather misleading statements.[19]

Walzel considers Lorck's term 'erlebte Rede' to be 'not very apt', but proposes no other. He drops completely Lorck's theory of a special poetic inspiration, and shows no sympathy with Lorck's attribution of a temporal function to the tense of 'erlebte Rede' statements. He himself approaches texts empirically, and he warmly recommends Herdin's dissertation of 1905, which had confined itself to the detection and description of the form in German writers—Wieland, Spielhagen, Fontane, Rosegger and others. Walzel points out that there are several transitional forms between simple indirect speech and 'erlebte Rede' that have long been normal in German writing, and that share with 'erlebte Rede' the lack of an introductory verb and of conjunctions—for instance, the indirect question with 'ob' ('Ob er heute kommen wird?'). But, Walzel goes on, 'erlebte Rede', the form that Herdin, Bally, and Lorck have discussed, is distinct from simple indirect speech since it does not have to submit to the subordinate word order (finite verb at the end of the clause), and since it substitutes the expressions of direct speech for the authorial language of indirect speech. Hence, Walzel maintains, it is wrong to consider 'erlebte Rede' a type of indirect speech. Walzel is not speaking about the hypothetical origin of 'erlebte Rede', but about its actual form, and Bally's identification of it as a type of indirect speech. His remarks are not unreasonable, though when, in *Gehalt und Gestalt,* he writes that 'erlebte Rede' 'has nothing to do with indirect speech' he is making a different and much more questionable assertion.

From this point Walzel's argument follows lines usual among German scholars of those days. He associates 'erlebte Rede' with direct speech, similar to the self-expression of a dramatic character, and calls it a type of mimicry, through which the reader 'experiences directly what the character in the narrative is experiencing'. Up to a point, all this defines the impact of 'erlebte Rede'. But Walzel sees this 'dramatic' form as the 'polar opposite' of the epic, narrative form. In adopting 'erlebte Rede', the author, he says, 'abandons his viewpoint', and with that his responsibility for what is said; the narrator abdicates before the character. 'Erlebte Rede' is thus the utter opposite of the narratorial account, and much more a challenge to the latter than direct speech; for since direct speech is enclosed in inverted commas and uses the first person, it demonstratively accepts a subordinate position in relation to the narrator's voice. In 'erlebte Rede', however, the character deposes, if only for a moment, the narrator. Walzel thus chimes in with those critics and writers who were speaking of 'the death of the narrator'. The chief difference from the more extreme of these is that Walzel does not agree that demise means an absolute advance, and, rather unresolutely, still stands up for the function of the story-teller, claiming that 'erlebte Rede' is not universally suitable, but appropriate only for certain types of narrative. In his remarks on Thomas Mann's new novel, *The Magic Mountain* (1924), we can see how welcome to him was the rather 'old-fashioned' prominence of the narrator in this work.

Like Lorck, Walzel does admit that 'erlebte Rede' occasionally reveals the ironic presence of the narrator, but his explanation is the inept one that, through the ironic tone, the author–narrator is merely conveying the fact that the words are not his. Such critical clumsiness illustrates the weakness of his general definition of 'erlebte Rede' as a dramatic, non-narrative form. He fails to observe the complex ways in which passages of 'erlebte Rede' are both technically integrated into a narrative and tinged (sometimes saturated) with narratorial comment. Did his failure to recognise this fusion of the character's viewpoint with the narrator's, this embodiment of the subjective perspective into the over-all structure of the narrative, this dual voice, arise from his failure to recognise the relationship of 'erlebte Rede' to indirect speech, or was the latter the result of the former? Walzel's references to Bally are indeed so slight that he scarcely seems to have occupied himself directly with his articles, and one even suspects a certain national prejudice. But of course, a scholar like other people may make innocent mistakes. Much of what Walzel wrote in these essays, and elsewhere, shows an observant and scrupulous mind. But in *Gehalt und Gestalt* he makes another naive mistake that has often been repeated. Distinguishing 'erlebte Rede' from inner monologue, he says that its syntax is different, since the inner monologue is conducted in the first person and the present tense, while 'erlebte Rede' requires the third person and not necessarily the present tense. Of course, this is true only of the theatrical monologue, which may be used in the novel, but need not be; the inner monologue of narrative fiction, conducted in the third person and an appropriate tense, is just as genuine an inner monologue. W. Hoffmeister puts it rightly when he says that 'erlebte Rede' is not identical with inner monologue but can be a constituent of it.[20]

Despite his reservations with regard to the term, Walzel like other German scholars found 'erlebte Rede' to be the most terse, convenient, and evocative of all the German replacements for 'style indirect libre', and it was soon generally adopted. In the article of 1928 by Leo Spitzer, quoted above ('On the origin of so-called "Erlebte Rede"'), this much-respected linguist also reluctantly accepted the term. He criticises both it and Lorck's analysis, on the grounds that both single out one side of the linguistic phenomenon, the expressive, subjective side, and do not do justice to its narratorial function. In Spitzer's view, the heart of the style is mimicry, and mimicry implies, as he states, both a person mimicked and a person mimicking. 'Erlebte Rede' is never without this authorial tinge or voice, and Spitzer points out that that is why it is often unclear whether a passage is objective (narratorial) narrative or subjective 'erlebte Rede'. In an earlier article

(*GRM*, IX, 1921), in which he had given examples of 'style indirect libre' from Italian literature, Spitzer had suggested the term 'pseudo-objektive Rede' ('pseudo-objective speech') for it. Now, in 1928, he is inclined to call it 'halbdirekte Rede' ('half-direct speech'), half way between direct speech and objective narrative; but without great zest, for he is ready to put up with 'erlebte Rede' because it is short, convenient, and already widely adopted.

In the same year Lerch, in his article 'Origin and significance of so-called "Erlebte Rede"', also bows to convenience. His reasons are different from Spitzer's, since he holds to his own term, 'Speech as fact'. But his chief criticism of Lorck's term seems to be its obscurity, and he quotes approvingly Werner Günther's complaint, which must have been often repeated since, that one does not know who is supposed to be doing the 'experiencing'—is it the author? the character? the reader? And isn't direct speech as much 'erlebt' as 'erlebte Rede'?

Most modern German critics who busy themselves with the concept seem to feel the same sort of doubts about the aptness of the term 'erlebte Rede', but use it because it is now established. Many use it without any clear notion of what it means, as a mere label; if definitions are essayed, they are often incomplete and may be misleading. Even Dorrit Cohn's and Ludwig Kahn's recent essays, and Werner Hoffmeister's study, circumspect as they are, are here and there faulty or inexact.[21] An examination of the use of the term 'erlebte Rede' would however try the patience of English readers too hard; here only enough has been said, it is hoped, to justify a refusal to import this term into English stylistics.

IV

Free indirect speech

There have been attempts at finding equivalents for 'erlebte Rede' in English—Dorrit Cohn for instance suggests 'narrated monologue'. Most English scholars use 'free indirect speech'. I too find this term the best, and will sum up my reasons, though these will be clear enough from the earlier discussion of 'style indirect libre' and 'erlebte Rede'.

The general difference between the French and German terms is that the former describes the supposed grammatical characteristics of the phenomenon, while the German describes its alleged psychological operation. I have already argued that 'erlebte Rede' does not correctly define the psychological function of the style. I would now go further and claim that this functioning is so intricate and complex a fusion of narratorial and subjective modes that it is impossible to find a name that would adequately designate it. For that reason a less ambitious title, confined to its grammatical features, is preferable, and likely to be less seriously misleading.

I have already shown that 'free' as it was originally used by Bally, namely, to indicate freedom from conjunctions and from introductory verb, is not a distinguishing feature of the device in all circumstances and languages. But it has already been suggested, and will become still more evident through the textual analyses, that Bally's 'style indirect libre' enjoys other and astonishing liberties—in the relation of the statement to the fictional character and narrator, in the tense-system, in the language, in the word-order (this latter particularly in German, where it disregards the normal requirement of the subordinate order). The qualifying adjective 'free' is therefore most appropriate, though in a different sense from that proposed by Bally.

'Indirect', as we have seen, was for Bally's critics the main stumbling block. The really effective aspect of the criticism of Lerch and Lorck was not, however, directed at the postulate that the form was a variety of indirect speech, but at the failure of this term to evoke the psychological impact of the form on the reader. If however we are ready to give up hope of defining the latter in a single, useful term, we can I believe be content with 'indirect'. The syntax of Bally's form, notably the transformation of the first person of direct speech to the third, and of the tense to conform with that of the introductory verb, belongs decisively to indirect speech. If there are exceptions, if as was argued the word-order is normal and not 'subordinate', it still seems better to ignore this minor variation and to call it 'indirect', rather than obliterate the relationship to indirect speech in general. The great value of the term 'indirect' is that it indicates that both a narrator and a character are involved. It also enjoys the advantage of attracting our attention to a relatively simple and obvious feature of the device, that can readily be recognised in a text, while 'erlebte Rede' is a very complex idea and not neat and plain enough for a signpost. It is only a pity that the term does not suggest the mingling, even fusion, of two voices in a dual voice, neither simple narrator nor simple character.

Lastly, 'speech' is adopted as the equivalent of Bally's 'style' simply because, in French, 'style' is used for *oratio* in the terms 'style direct' and 'style indirect', and Bally's term is intended to assert a relationship with these. English uses 'speech' for the same purpose (just as German uses 'Rede'). For some time I myself preferred the name 'free indirect style', since it seemed to me that 'speech' too strongly suggested that we are here concerned with the literary expression of spoken words or articulate thoughts; 'style', the French term, has in this respect a useful ambiguity. But the term 'speech' in these contexts refers not to actual spoken language, but to a mode of discourse, and it is important to use for 'free indirect speech' the same term as for 'direct speech' and 'indirect speech', since they are all in fact so closely bound together. 'Free indirect speech' it is then, and I may be excused for using the abbreviation FIS.

PART 2

Texts

The following texts are intended to provide typical examples of the uses of free indirect speech, and to enable us to examine both its internal structure and the stylistic and narrative contexts in which it functions. Our examples are taken from English, French, and German literature of the nineteenth century, with a single excursion into Russian. While we may expect our conclusions to be valid for the modern Indo-European languages, it is clear that the form of free indirect speech is bound up with a specific type of language, and no inferences can be made as regards other language families.

The studies are arranged in a historical sequence. This does not mean that a history of the incidence of FIS is being attempted. Such a project would be an enormous task, would certainly include some medieval texts, and might begin with classical Greek. To conceive of a history also invites a misunderstanding. For, although the form crops up here and there since the Middle Ages, there is until modern times, after Flaubert, no continuous tradition of its use and transmission as a literary technique; until Flaubert no writer seems to have used it with a clear consciousness of its stylistic identity and meaning. So that, though one can observe its appearance in this or that author since the Renaissance, one cannot draw a graph of a tradition or of an evolution from crude beginnings to artistic accomplishment. Indeed, when it first appears as a prominent and continuous feature in a novel, in Goethe and Jane Austen, it is already used with the greatest skill and propriety. This fact alone seems to suggest that, with such slight literary antecedents, there must be some linguistic habit in common usage on which these authors were drawing.

However, the roughly chronological arrangement of these chapters has a historical significance. First, as has often been observed, the growing and extended use of FIS is an instrument and symptom of the evolution of the novel towards the depiction of states of mind, temperament, moods, rather than external actions. But we can also observe a technical evolution of the device. There are at the beginning a number of awkwardnesses, stylistic, grammatical, or merely typographical, that disappear with time. There is also an extension of its range that accompanies its growing familiarity, and that provokes or assumes an astonishing imaginative agility in the reader. For the linguist it focuses some aspects of the problem of the validity of traditional grammar.

The texts all belong to the period before free indirect speech became widespread and fashionable. I wished to investigate the discovery of its resources, and this was certainly simpler and clearer in the earlier

34

authors, and could be analysed with greater confidence. So I did not include Henry James, in whose work it is triumphantly established, nor of course the later accomplishment of Proust or Joyce or their generation, with their stylistic audacities. In any case, its appearance among them is much better known.

It is clear that writers, when they have used free indirect speech, have done so with a precise intuitive understanding of its syntax. Normally they will not have had any theoretical consciousness of its distinctiveness, and certainly not of its grammatical structure. That it was little used by certain authors or in certain periods cannot be attributed to lack of literary skill. One of the reasons for its infrequent use in the eighteenth century (before Rousseau's *Emile*) must have been the unpreparedness of the reading public, and one of the first signs of its recognition as a stylistic form arose from an author's awareness that it might be misunderstood. It occurs in Fielding's *Joseph Andrews* (1742), where otherwise FIS appears only in scraps of mimicry of a character's personal idiom. When, in book 3, chapter 2, Parson Adams and his fellow travellers are given shelter by hospitable but suspicious people, Adams proves his scholarly identity by a great monological discourse on Homer, to which his host listens in mute and admiring astonishment. At his host's request Adams, put into rare good spirits by an excellent meal, then tells the story of Joseph's misfortunes, and earns from his host further praise for his story-telling. Adams then asks his host to 'return the favour' and tell the story of his own life:

> Adams told him it was now in his power to return that favour; for his extraordinary goodness as well as that fund of literature he was master of, which he did not expect to find under such a roof, had raised in him more curiosity [. . .]

To this Fielding, in the second edition, appended a footnote:

> The author has by some been represented to have made a blunder here, for Adams had, indeed, shown some learning, say they, perhaps all the author had; but the gentleman [the host] has shown none, unless his approbation of Mr. Adams be such: but surely it would be preposterous in him to call it such.

Fielding goes on seemingly to admit his error, excusing its retention in the second edition on the grounds that it is a beauty-spot.

The note is pure spoof, of course. It is not the author who says that the host is a scholar, but Adams in his simplicity and warmth of feeling, and the passage is a neat bit of free indirect speech: and Fielding is laughing at the readers who failed to recognise it. Perhaps this difficulty, however, discouraged him from using FIS? Modern writers have not been so considerate to their readers, in spite of the fact that there are many examples in critical writings of misunderstandings due to a failure to recognise the form.

Textual studies require to be based on the original text, and particularly in the case of free indirect speech, since the character of a statement may be decisively established by idiomatic usages of different kinds, a particular tense, certain particles, slight stylistic nuances, that sometimes cannot be rendered in another language or require quite different means. But some of the major features of free indirect speech are perfectly reproducible in translation, and for the sake of readers who are not familiar with the foreign languages discussed here I have translated the passages used, and in my comments have referred as far as possible to the translations. The original texts are of course also given, as some features occur only in them, and in any case they will allow readers to check the translation. Quite skilful translations may indeed, for the sake of a more natural or elegant English, evade or obscure the particular stylistic feature for which I quoted a passage; bad translations may often obliterate it altogether. For this reason I have not used published translations, not even those that in general are perfectly adequate (though I refer to them in the Notes), with one exception. Apart from this exception, all the translations are my own, so that I could ensure the accuracy of the translation in respect to those aspects of the text to which I wished to draw attention; sometimes I have had to sacrifice elegance to literalness. The exception is D. Magarshack's translation of Dostoyevsky's *The Idiot,* a far finer translation than I could aspire to; and in this case I have not published the Russian text, since so few readers, alas, would be able to use it. This translation has, I hope, served my purpose, and I have tried, without using Russian, to indicate as clearly as possible where translation from Russian is forced to be at a loss.

V

Early accomplishment

Goethe: *The Elective Affinities*

There are isolated examples of FIS in Goethe's *Wilhelm Meister's Apprenticeship* and the editorial ending of *The Sorrows of Young Werther*, but in these earlier novels they are only occasional. In *The Elective Affinities* (*Die Wahlverwandtschaften*, 1809) FIS is a recurring mode of narration and helps to establish the whole tone of the novel.

In several ways the narrative procedures are what we might call old-fashioned, even clumsy. Information may be provided for the reader through unlikely conversations. The characters are scarcely differentiated by their mode of speech. The narrator has a double role. Usually he is non-personal, anonymous, and thus can claim access to the innermost thoughts of the characters and the most private events (though we cannot call him 'omniscient', since certain areas and persons are much better known to him than others, while Ottilie's spiritual crisis remains as much a mystery for him as for the characters). But, incompatibly, he appears at times to be an elderly friend of the family, with a personal sympathy that leads him often to express comments of approval or disapproval, and sometimes to write of Ottilie as 'the dear child', 'the heavenly child', or in some similarly affectionate phrase. Sometimes he writes from within the consciousness of a character, as we shall see; but sometimes he takes up a position outside the group, for instance describing what a 'picturesque' group they form on occasion. From time to time he may address the reader direct with the editorial 'we', perhaps asking the sort of question—'For whom did Eduard do this?'—that older story-tellers asked their listeners in order to ensure their attention, stir their expectancy, and take a fresh breath.

But Goethe's theme of emotional and moral entanglement is a boldly modern one, and its modernity is matched by the bold and frequent use of a stylistic innovation. Free indirect speech constantly accompanies the story, enriching the narrator's perspective with that of the characters. It is used for all the four main characters, and even occurs within the inset tale told by the English milord. These FIS passages often convey irony or sympathy (or both), that is, they bear the tone of the narrator as well as the character. Sometimes they are neutral, and the irony itself may be only implicit, since it often arises from the simple contradiction between the outcome of events and the false hopes and self-delusion of the characters, their errors of judgement, errors that inevitably belong to the uncertainties of the present moment. There are few examples of FIS in the early chapters of the novel, and they become numerous only after the 'elective affinities' announce their presence and begin to play havoc with the lives of the four chief characters (with and after book I, chapter 10).[22]

As in almost all novels, it is sometimes impossible to decide with certainty whether some passages are narratorial-objective or free indirect speech; there may be nothing in the grammatical form, linguistic style, or the content, to make it certain. In *The Elective Affinities* the uncertainty is more likely because the characters scarcely have a characteristic mode of expression, a personal, idiosyncratic style. There is, it is true, more energy in the Captain's thought and speech, a distinctive rational clarity and feminine maturity, even sophistication, in Charlotte's, impetuosity, passion, and frivolity in Eduard's, and a gentle reticence in Ottilie's; these qualities find expression more through sentence structure than vocabulary. Their language, in conversations, letters, diary, and thoughts, is a stylised version of that of educated polite society, the language the narrator shares with them. To identify the personal source of a statement we depend, more than in modern novels, on the content rather than on the manner. In fact, the events of the story and the narratorial descriptions of behaviour differentiate the characters much more subtly and clearly than the style—Ottilie's characteristic gesture, as described by the narrator, is infinitely more speaking than the way she speaks or writes, while the excerpts from her diary are stylistically indistinguishable from the narrator's prose. The occasional obtrusiveness of the narrator in his personalised role, his personal and sentimental participation, also contribute to the uncertainty, in some cases, as to the attribution of a statement, whether to narrator or character.

But there are helpful indicators, and it may be useful to sum them up systematically.

1. We find, very occasionally, temporal or spatial indicators that indubitably refer us to the time and place at which the character stands, and establish the typical character-perspective of FIS:

Ottile, who had not yet finished the copy that was so urgently
needed for early tomorrow, . . .

Ottilie, die mit ihrer auf morgen früh so nötigen Abschrift noch
nicht fertig war, . . . (Part I, chapter 12, 103).[23]

'Tomorrow', which in direct speech can only be used with a present or
future tense, in simple indirect speech would here be rendered as 'the
next day' with the past tense. That it is combined with the past tense
is typical FIS, since it aligns the narrator with the temporal situation
of the character. Though 'now' and the more common spatial indicators like 'here' do not bear so unambiguous a subjective reference
as some other deictic adverbs, 'now' ('jetzt') and 'here' ('hier') do so in
certain contexts (pp. 131, 141). Particles that indicate emotional reservations and logical arguments within the character frequently announce the presence of FIS—'surely', 'yet', 'yes, but', 'alas'—'gewiss',
'doch', 'ja doch', 'doch gewiss', 'leider', 'ach' (I, 13, 109; I, 10, 87; II,
13, 266; II, 10, 235; II, 9, 231). Not always. For while the 'alas' of II,
9, 231 clearly informs us that it expresses Ottilie's regret and is FIS,
two forms of 'alas' ('leider' and 'ach') in II, 13, 172–3 express the
narrator's concern, and are instances of the somewhat confusing inter-
polation of the personalised narrator.

2. Some of these particles heighten the exclamatory nature of the
statement to which they belong, and, generally, exclamations and
exclamatory questions often introduce and sustain passages of FIS.
They may constitute the sole FIS utterances in an otherwise purely
narratorial passage. So, when Eduard is re-reading the letter in
which he is announcing his readiness to renounce his love for Ottilie
and even not to resist the healing effects of absence, two separate
exclamatory sentences, each with a tell-tale subjective verb of
obligation—'was to' ('sollte')—introduce and confirm the FIS
perspective in a paragraph at the outset narratorial:

> This last expression flowed out of his pen, not his heart. Yes,
> as he saw it on paper he began bitterly to weep. In one way or
> another he was to renounce the happiness, yes the unhappiness,
> of loving Ottilie! Only now did he feel what he was doing. He
> was leaving without knowing what the outcome might be. Now,
> at least, he was not to see her; whether he would ever see her
> again, what certainty could he promise himself about that?

> Diese letzte Wendung floss ihm aus der Feder, nicht aus dem
> Herzen. Ja, wie er sie auf dem Papier sah, fing er bitterlich zu

weinen an. Er sollte auf irgend eine Weise dem Glück, ja dem Unglück, Ottilien zu lieben, entsagen! Jetzt erst fühlte er was er tat. Er entfernte sich, ohne zu wissen, was daraus entstehen konnte. Er sollte sie wenigstens jetzt nicht wiedersehen; ob er sie je wiedersähe, welche Sicherheit konnte er sich darüber versprechen? (I, 16, 131).

In German, the simple past tense does for both preterite and past imperfect. Usually, 'er entfernte sich' would mean 'he left'. But here it means that he was conscious that he would be leaving, and is part of a FIS statement. In French it would be typically put in the imperfect, and in this context English too can properly use the imperfect 'he was leaving'.

Ottilie's reflections as she considers how changed all is since the year before are given in a series of exclamations (II, 9, 231), as are Charlotte's when she is courageously arguing with herself against the likelihood of disaster (II, 10, 235–6). Often FIS may be more simply suggested by the intonation of an exclamatory 'such' or 'so'—'such a rich harvest' ('so reichliche Ernte', I, 17, 138); Charlotte's thought that Eduard was 'so charming, so friendly, so pressing' (I, 9, 101) or Ottilie's reflections about herself, in the third person and past tense, that 'she had never been so rich and never so poor' (II, 9, 231). Since the narrator occasionally uses exclamations of this type to express authorial concern, we cannot assume that they always belong to FIS, just as the 'Yes' that opens the second sentence of the passage quoted above belongs more to the narrator than to Eduard (while the 'yes' in the following line is Eduard's, and indicates FIS).

3. Frequently the presence of FIS is revealed by auxiliary verbs like 'ought' or 'should' ('sollen', 'dürfen'), which may refer to a supposition of obligation or permission on the part of the character, rather than to an objective obligation. The presence of 'was to' ('sollte') in combination with the exclamatory form in two sentences of the passage quoted securely establishes them as FIS. So also in

What changes were not bound to be brought about here by the different times of day, by moon and sun!

Was mussten nicht hier die verschiedenen Tageszeiten, was Mond und Sonne für Wirkungen hervorbringen!

The typical combination of deictic 'here', exclamatory form, and the obligation 'were bound to be brought' indicates that this necessity is not objective, but a self-persuading wish of Charlotte's. It is interesting that Goethe uses the indicative mood of 'mussten', not the tempting subjunctive 'müssten', appreciating the difference between indirect speech with the subjunctive and free indirect speech.

4. Sometimes we read a passage as FIS, to find at the end that a narratorial explanation, like 'he thought' or 'such were his/her observations', is appended as if to assure us that the observations are indeed by a character. Bally considered such cases and concluded that the addition of the *verbum dicendi* or *credendi* in this form did not make such a passage any less an example of free indirect speech. The experience of reading bears this view out; under all such circumstances the passage produces a livelier and more vigorous effect than simple indirect speech.

5. So far attention has been directed towards the subjective side of free indirect speech, the ways in which a statement, grammatically in narratorial form, asserts its provenance in the consciousness of the character. But in these passages there is also a narratorial voice. Many of them have an ironical flavour, even if the irony arises only out of the contrast between the character's hopes and expectations and the actual outcome of events. The opportunity that FIS provides for delicate, subtle irony is illustrated in the final paragraph of chapter 14 in book I, at the conclusion of the (narratorial) account of Eduard's search through old ledgers for the date on which, when a boy, he had planted a copse of plane trees. The narrative is conducted here, as in a few other parts of the novel, in the present tense, so that this tense governs the parts in indirect speech also:

> He leafs through a few volumes; the entry is found: but how astonished, how delighted Eduard is when he notices the most marvellous coincidence. The day, the year of the planting of the trees is the very same day and year of Ottilie's birth.

> Er durchblättert einige Bände; der Umstand findet sich; aber wie erstaunt, wie erfreut ist Eduard, als er das wunderbarste Zusammentreffen bemerkt. Der Tag, das Jahr jener Baumpflanzung ist zugleich der Tag, das Jahr von Ottiliens Geburt. (I, 14, 118).

That the coincidence is 'most marvellous' is of course Eduard's thought, not the narrator's, for the latter on other occasions comments explicitly on Eduard's foolish hankering after signs and wonders to guarantee his happiness. 'The most marvellous coincidence' is as it were a quotation from Eduard, and it is his voice that is heard in the

41

following exclamatory sentence, that closes the chapter with a flourish. But not his voice alone. The choice of words, the excited exclamatory tone, betray another, evaluating voice that guides our judgement.

The wishful thinking that Eduard, Charlotte, the Captain, and Ottilie all occasionally indulge in is often described in FIS, and one can observe a double result. Statements in this form exert a stronger persuasive force upon the reader than narratorial description or simple indirect speech, since the presence and emotive concern of the character are more immediately felt; they are also more powerful than direct speech, since FIS is less clearly marked as the mere view of a character and, since it so smoothly fits into the narrative, seems to bear some guarantee or recommendation from the narrator (it was this effect that led Lerch to suggest the designation 'Speech as fact' for it). But, on the other hand, the fact that the self-delusion remains only implicit makes the irony all the more penetrating.[24]

This irony is complex. Sometimes it has the sharp note of criticism, but very often it is mixed with sympathy; sometimes the character's error or self-delusion is so deeply rooted in essential character and the inevitable ambiguity of life that the irony is wholly sympathetic and approaches tragic pathos. On the two occasions on which FIS is used to express Charlotte's thoughts about her husband's nightly visit, it sympathetically shows her coming to terms with the unease it arouses (for she knows each was using the other as a substitute). Eduard's feeling of guilt, when he awakes in the morning, is reported narratorially, and so is the fact that Charlotte wakes to find that her husband has already left her. But this last fact is accompanied by the words 'strangely enough' ('seltsam genug'), and this must be Charlotte's thought, not the narrator's observation, for he has already told us that Eduard has gone. There is a touch of irony here but, left without further comment, it suggests a deeper puzzlement and apprehension than Charlotte wishes to be conscious of (I, 11, 101–2). The arguments with which Charlotte later tries to persuade herself that things will turn out well, and the practical plans she makes, are not ironical in any usual sense, and can be called so only in the sense that the reader knows them to be illusory (II, 10, 235–6, 236–7).

Above all in Ottilie's case, the general benevolence of the narrator—and indeed of the older people—to the 'dear child' extends also to the FIS employed to reflect her thought. Her reflections on the great change in her life since she arrived at the mansion are only sympathetically tinged, just as the thoughts that follow, imagining the happy future of Charlotte's baby, though soon to be shown to be tragically false, are presented without irony of any kind (II, 9, 231–2). On the other hand, there is an overt if affectionate irony in almost all the FIS connected with Eduard—for instance, his overweening confidence that the tangled relationships will easily be unravelled:

> All the parties needed only to consent to what they desired; a divorce would certainly be granted; they would soon be married, and Eduard planned to go travelling with Ottilie.

> Alle Teile brauchten nur in das zu willigen, was sie wünschten; eine Scheidung war gewiss zu erlangen; eine baldige Verbindung sollte folgen, und Eduard wollte mit Ottilien reisen. (II, 13, 266).

The brevity and clarity of his argument, the confidence of his logic, insinuate the irony.

FIS so frequently serves the narrator's ironical purpose, not only in *The Elective Affinities* but with many authors who use the device, that some critics have considered irony a constant function of it. But Dorrit Cohn is nearer the truth when she claims that it can bear either an ironical or a lyrical tone, lyrical here meaning something close to what I have called 'sympathetic'. It would not be hard to distinguish a more complex range of narratorial comment implicitly expressed through FIS, but these distinctions are not so important as a more fundamental observation, namely, that free indirect speech is never purely and simply the evocation of a character's thought and perception, but always bears, in its vocabulary, its intonation, its syntactical composition and other stylistic features, in its content, or its context, or in some combination of these, the mark of the narrator.

6. In *The Elective Affinities* FIS is used almost always for the reproduction of a character's thoughts; only very rarely does it interpret actual speech, and when it does so, Goethe's handling is not very lively or mobile (e.g. I, 17, 138; II, 7, 212). FIS may occur, as we have seen, in odd phrases, sentences, and snatches in association with other forms, but sometimes it may form longer passages, such as Ottilie's reflections (II, 9, 231) or Charlotte's self-argument (II, 10, 236). It is impossible to deny these longer passages the name of inner monologue. Their grammar is of course different from that of the soliloquy in the theatre, since the first person and present tense of the latter are replaced in the novel by the normal form of indirect speech, the third person and the tense dictated by the introductory verb (usually the past).

7. Throughout the novel, the thoughts of the characters are given in a fully articulated form; the narrator usually makes a coherent and logical sequence out of them. Since the main characters belong to a cultured social group accustomed to converse, this ready verbalisation does not as a rule seem forced, especially since the expression of the characters' thoughts is rarely prolonged, and is often interrupted by narratorial observations, description of behaviour and events, etc. There is, however, at least one instance that suggests that Goethe felt that FIS could express something deeper in the psyche than could take shape as a conscious thought.

When Eduard receives the document that Ottilie has copied for him and observes that her handwriting grows more and more like his own (in the original document), his delight is only marred by regret that it is a mere business document:

> O, would that it were a different document! he says silently to himself; and yet, even so, it is the fairest assurance that his highest wish is fulfilled. For, after all, it remains in his hands, and will he not for ever more press it to his heart, though disfigured by the signature of a third party!

> O dass es ein andres Dokument wäre! sagt er sich im stillen; und doch ist es ihm auch so schon die schönste Versicherung, dass sein höchster Wunsch erfüllt sei. Bleibt es ja doch in seinen Händen, und wird er es nicht immerfort an sein Herz drücken, obgleich entstellt durch die Unterschrift eines Dritten! (I, 13, 108–9).

As Goethe does not use inverted commas at all in this novel, their absence here has no particular significance; also, the use of the present tense for indirect speech is simply due to the fact that from the beginning of this chapter the narrator has adopted the present tense. The meaning is clear. The first exclamatory sentence is direct speech; it is a complete, articulated thought. It is not certain whether the following sentence, from 'and yet', is intended to be narratorial or free indirect speech. The rest is indubitably FIS; the exclamatory form, the self-directed argument indicated by 'after all' ('ja doch'), the lover's extravagance of 'for ever more' ('immerfort'), the slightly absurd sensitivity of 'disfigured' ('entstellt'), all proclaim the fact. What is the difference between these FIS statements and the direct speech that opens the passage? I believe there is a difference in kind. The first is a clear thought; but the FIS gives a different sort of mental activity. It communicates Eduard's emotion and the sort of words that occur to him, but we hardly feel that these sentences are formed thus in his mind. What they do is to sum up confused and excited processes in an intricate, even tortuous syntactical form, so that through this complex structure we have a glimpse of those pre-articulate mental processes that precede literate consciousness. I believe that Goethe is here using FIS as an instrument for the recording of a level of awareness that cannot properly be put into words in the form of direct speech or narratorial explanation, and that even seems to resist grammatical and literate expression altogether. We may recognise it as an early attempt on the way towards the achievement of James Joyce and his generation, intermediate stages being marked by Büchner and Dostoyevsky.

It is surprising to find so many features of free indirect speech present in Goethe's novel and already used with easy accomplishment. We might be equally surprised by Jane Austen's novels. If the question is asked: How could this come about? some part of an answer suggests itself. These novels are centrally concerned with the adjustments to one another of a small group of people belonging to the same social class, shaped by the same education, and permeated by the same cultural presuppositions. The main issue is the establishment or dislocation of true, sincere, personal relationships; what they do is only important in relation to the intentions and feelings that promote and accompany the actions. Hence the author's urgent need to evoke thought-processes as the characters themselves know them, the image of the world round them and its driving forces as it exists in their mind and imagination.

Jane Austen

Jane Austen's novels supply the preconditions one might consider necessary for the unhampered emergence of free indirect speech. They focus upon a small group of people who belong to one class and one cultural world, whose values, feelings, and thoughts, even if unknown, contain no mystery for them or for the narrator. They do not lack plot, but the plot consists almost entirely of the changing attitudes of the characters to one another, so that their thoughts and feelings are the structural elements of the story. There is a narrator who is prominent as story-teller and moralist, but who is (with rare lapses) non-personal, non-defined, and therefore may enjoy access to the most secret privacy of the characters. So truly is this impersonal narrator the 'spirit of the story', that one cannot ascribe him/her a sex, and it is misleading to use either 'him' or 'her' for this function; I use 'him' throughout this study in the same way as one uses 'man' for 'mankind' (in Jane Austen's case it usefully makes a clearer distinction between the author and the narrator). One might be tempted to call this non-personal narrator 'omniscient', but in fact his omniscience is in evidence only in regard to the main characters, the others—including as a rule the disagreeable ones—moving at different places in the penumbra outside the main beam of the narrator's searchlight. From the beginning, the narrator aligns his perspective with the central characters, those on whom our attention and sympathy are to be directed. There is throughout great emphasis on what the characters think and feel, and this is made manifest through liberal servings of conversation and also through narratorial descriptions of their thoughts, often combined with moral commentary.[25] Thus FIS, the reproduction in indirect form of their speech and thought, fits very naturally into the general character and purpose of the novels.

Jane Austen's free indirect speech is much more vivacious than Goethe's, partly because it is used much more often to render speech and the tone of speech than in *The Elective Affinities*. We often note a peculiar typographical convention. In *Sense and Sensibility* (1811), the first novel Jane Austen published, we find:[26]

> When he [John Dashwood] gave his promise to his father, he meditated within himself to increase the fortunes of his sisters by the present of a thousand pounds a-piece. He then really thought himself equal to it. The prospect of four thousand a year [...] warmed his heart. —'Yes, he would give them three thousand pounds: it would be liberal and handsome. Three thousand pounds! he could spare so considerable a sum with little inconvenience.' He thought about it all day long.

The sentences placed within inverted commas bear typical FIS indicators, the exclamations 'Yes' and 'Three thousand pounds', and are couched in the phraseology of the character, as the preceding narratorial sentences are not. They belong indeed to FIS. That they are placed within inverted commas does not mean that they are spoken, of course, but only that they are Dashwood's thoughts. The use of the inverted commas is doubly interesting. It shows that the author was aware of the difference between this stylistic form and others, for instance simple indirect speech or narratorial description; and further, it shows that the author was aware of its nearness to direct speech, even though the third person is used. We find a similar use of inverted commas in many novelists, for instance in Walter

Scott, Balzac, and Stendhal, and it offers an interesting contribution to the debate on whether free indirect speech belongs more to direct or to indirect speech. In this particular passage we note too that FIS is used to denote a stage in John Dashwood's ruminations, at the point when his vague ponderings reach the level of clear thought and decision.

A slightly different implication is borne by a similar use in Walter Scott's *The Heart of Mid-Lothian* (chapter 4, Penguin edition, p. 45):

> The usual hour for producing the criminal had been past for many minutes, yet the spectators observed no symptom of his appearance. 'Would they venture to defraud public justice?' was the question men began anxiously to ask at each other. The first answer in every case was bold and positive—'They dare not.'

The question, though placed in inverted commas, is clearly FIS, since the conditional 'would' is used instead of the future 'will'; the answer, 'They dare not', is direct speech. Why the distinction? I think because the FIS form of the question suggests that many questions were asked, and only their gist is given here; it transmits the feeling of bewilderment and anxiety in the crowd. The direct speech of the answer suggests unanimity and confidence. We shall often find that FIS passages suggest not so much an actual speech but the gist, a résumé, even though the character's own personal idiom is retained.

The use of inverted commas is one of the rare signs we can find of an author's awareness of the distinctiveness of this stylistic form. Typically, it betrays a certain unsureness about its status as between direct and indirect speech. This unsureness prevails too in the related case of the inner monologue, for throughout the nineteenth century and into the twentieth, in e.g. Balzac, Stendhal, and Fontane, or Faulkner and J.-P. Sartre, inner monologues are often placed within inverted commas, though these cannot mean that the monologues are spoken. Perhaps it is all chiefly a typographical problem. And though it is true that the more sophisticated modern readership can dispense with typographical indicators, many perplexed readers of modern novels might well be glad of such reading-aids.

There is a related unclarity in Jane Austen's use of FIS. It often occurs as a substitute for direct speech, often freely mingled with pieces of direct speech; but sometimes we are uncertain whether it reproduces thoughts or actual spoken words. One example among many:[27]

> Mrs. Dashwood did not at all approve of what her husband intended to do for his sisters. To take three thousand pounds from

the fortune of their dear little boy, would be impoverishing him to the most dreadful degree. She begged him to think again on the subject. How could he answer it to himself to rob his child, and his only child too, of so large a sum? And what possible claim could the Miss Dashwoods, who were related to him only by half blood, which she considered no relationship at all, have on his generosity to so large an amount. It was very well known that no affection was ever supposed to exist between the children of any man by different marriages; and why was he to ruin himself, and their poor little Harry, by giving away all his money to his half sisters?

All this is excellent and vivacious FIS, full of Mrs Dashwood's tone, expressions, and distortions, and of the narrator's irony. It leads directly on to:

'It was my father's last request to me,' replied her husband, 'that I should assist his widow and daughters.'

The conversation then continues in direct speech.

So, though there is no unambiguous indication in the text that the opening passage is part of a conversation, we are meant to understand it so, that is, as the reproduction in FIS of a harangue by Mrs Dashwood. Without this context we should, I think, take it as a summary account of many thoughts and arguments going round in Mrs Dashwood's head, over a period, a gradual marshalling of her position, not merely one argument with her husband. Its liveliness, persuasiveness, intonations, exaggerations are perhaps more than a single confrontation would require. Or, if we accept that it is a speech in a conversation, then her loquacity, unscrupulousness, her parentheses, etc. suggest an obsessiveness almost Dickensian in quality. I am not sure that the latter is intended and feel that here there is a failure, very rare in Jane Austen, to use FIS with precision.

Quite often, in this early period, an author feels it to be advisable to help out the FIS with a 'he thought', 'he felt', etc., where a later author could count on its being recognised without explicit verbs. This occurs often in Jane Austen's novels; I quote however an example from Walter Scott because it exemplifies something else too. It is from *The Heart of Mid-Lothian,* chapter 31, when Jeanie, on her pilgrimage to London, meets the mad and disreputable Madge Wildfire, from whom she hopes for help:

Jeanie sighed heavily to think that it should be her lot on the Lord's day, and during kirk-time too, to parade the street of an inhabited village with so very grotesque a comrade; but necessity had no law, since, without a positive quarrel with the madwoman, which, in the circumstances, would have been very inadvisable, she could see no means of shaking herself free of her society.

The word 'parade', the attitude to the Lord's day and kirk-time, are characteristic enough of Jeanie for this FIS to need no 'to think'. But the tense of 'necessity had no law' is curious, and invites comment. It is of course due to its belonging to indirect speech, governed by 'sighed to think'. But the past tense 'had' reads oddly, and it would seem that Scott here has fallen a victim to grammatical propriety. For the present tense in general saws does not indicate time, it has a universalist, non-temporal meaning. If in indirect speech the present is changed into the past, this tense inevitably does give it a temporal meaning; it now seems to be a thought of the character devised in this particular situation, and therefore almost an excuse; it loses its claim to absolute truth. We read in it here a pretext that Jeanie invents to justify her behaviour, rather than an objective justification of it. Scott meant it to appear as her thought, of course, but did not wish, I believe, to suggest any subterfuge on her part. It is probable, however, that a generalisation like 'necessity knows no law' is never used in the past tense, except with an ironic implication. In such a case, as in the examples given below from George Eliot, Trollope, and Flaubert, the writer is faced not with a choice between what is grammatically right or wrong but with stylistic alternatives bearing different insinuations.[28]

Many such problems arise in the transposition of direct speech into indirect, particularly in the replacement of this univeralist 'present' tense by the past, and the replacement of the first or second person by the third. It is, for example, impossible to turn ejaculations like 'My God!' or 'Just think!' into the third-person form required for both simple and free indirect speech.[29]

After these preliminary remarks, it is time to turn to the great accomplishment of Jane Austen's use of free indirect speech. I will confine my examples to *Mansfield Park* (1814).[30] Graham Hough, in his admirable analysis of what he calls 'objective narrative' in *Emma*, makes a necessary distinction between author and narrator, authorial voice and objective narrative.[31] He notes that the author herself, Jane Austen, assets herself very occasionally as a personal judgement, but that this 'authorial' voice is so rare as to be 'negligible'. This all applies to *Mansfield Park*. In the last chapter the author drops the mask of the narrator and appears *in propria persona:* 'Let other pens dwell on guilt and misery. I quit such odious subjects as soon as I can, impatient to restore everybody, not greatly in fault themselves, to tolerable comfort, and to have done with the rest.' This frank intervention causes no confusion. But there is a more subtle case.

At the end of chapter 1, after we have been told of Mrs Price's surprise at Fanny's translation to Mansfield Park, we read: 'Poor woman! she probably thought change of air might agree with many of her children.' With this exclamation of sympathy, the narrator has acquired something of a personality, and in accordance with this, the qualifying 'probably' renounces the usual narratorial right of omniscience. It looks as if we can say that here the author, Jane Austen, for a moment replaces the non-personal narrator, in the way that is not uncommon in the earlier novel, of Fielding or Goethe, and is much indulged in by Thackeray. In himself, the personalised, obtrusive narrator can be an admirable medium for a certain type of novel, as we can see with Cervantes or Fielding. But in novels where FIS is used to any extent, this personalised narrator can be a source of confusion, especially since his observations are frequently signalled by the same sort of indicators as the subjective statements of FIS (in the above case, the exclamation and the 'probably'.) His appearance also chimes in ill with the omniscience of the impersonal narrator. Thackeray and Trollope provide repeated examples of a confusion that, in Jane Austen's case, only momentarily blurs the focus.

Jane Austen's objective narrator in *Mansfield Park* uses various means to convey the thoughts and feelings of the characters. There are extensive psychological descriptions and explanations, and these are frequently built out with direct speech. Occasionally thoughts are presented as if they were spoken—e.g. Fanny's long rumination after the receipt of the troubling letter from Mary Crawford (III, 13, 424–5). In all these forms, the narrator is a necessary presence, even if only as a reporter of direct speech. There is also an occasional passage of simple indirect speech, which can turn into a clumsy and toneless instrument, an introductory verb governing many clauses linked by 'that . . . that . . . and that . . .' (II, 8, 256).

In addition to these forms we find much free indirect speech. There is often lively mimicry in these passages, with an ironic reproduction of the typical words and intonations of a character, as in the passage quoted above from *Sense and Sensibility*. Professor Hough is wrong, however, to say that FIS entails the use of the *ipsissima verba* of a character. While it may do so, it often does so only partly, as we shall observe. Professor Hough also wrongly states that it occurs 'in brief snatches'. It usually does so, but there are also longer passages. In his analysis, however, Hough comes to a conclusion of great importance. He demonstrates that the view of a character, when presented in FIS, has only a qualified validity in respect to truth, wins from the reader only a qualified assent (if at all), and is always subordinate in status to 'the narrator's objective judgement', which remains 'firmly in charge' wherever it occurs—judgement here referring to facts as well as to moral evaluations. I believe this to be true of FIS throughout the nineteenth century.

The context is always of decisive importance in determining what function a piece of FIS fulfils. For instance, it often occurs within a passage of dialogue, in close association with direct speech, and in this context it bears a meaning as a contrast to direct speech. When Fanny first comes to Mansfield Park, and is wretched, Edmund is the first to console here. He says to her, 'You are sorry to leave Mamma, my dear little Fanny' and so forth, and ends by inviting her to 'tell me all about your brothers and sisters'. Her answers are given first in simple indirect speech, then in FIS, and finally in direct speech (I, 2, 15–16):

> On pursuing the subject, he found that dear as all these brothers and sisters generally were, there was one among them who ran more in her thoughts than the rest. It was William whom she talked of most and wanted most to see. William, the eldest, a year older than herself, her constant companion and friend; her advocate with her mother (of whom he was the darling) in every distress. 'William did not like she should come away—he had told her he should miss her very much indeed.' 'But William will write to you, I dare say.' 'Yes, he had promised he would, but he had told *her* to write first.' 'And when shall you do it?' She hung her head and answered, hesitatingly, 'she did not know; she had not any paper.'

Edmund's remarks are always in direct speech; hers are first explained by the narrator, and then presented in free indirect speech (though placed within inverted commas). The psychological effect is marked. At first the narrator is her interpreter, and when her own words are given, they only have FIS form; we are thus made to feel her modesty and shyness, for it seems that the words have to be coaxed out of her. Even when she speaks up, she seems hardly able to look at Edmund, and can hardly arrogate the self-assertive 'I' for herself. And, as from this point the conversation then proceeds in direct speech on both sides (though Fanny remains very reticent), we actually experience her growth of confidence and trust in the very form of the dialogue.

Elsewhere, FIS used within conversations may serve different functions. In the first chapter the narrator makes it explicit that Mrs Norris is selfish and hypocritical, and Sir Thomas Bertram indolent and hesitant. In their talks over the adoption of Fanny, FIS is reserved particularly for those stages at which one or the other is taking refuge in evasions:

> Sir Thomas could not give so instantaneous and unqualified a consent. He debated and hesitated;—it was a serious charge;—a girl so brought up must be adequately provided for, otherwise there would be cruelty instead of kindness in taking her from her family. He thought of his own four children—of his two sons—of cousins in love, etc;—but no sooner had he deliberately begun to state his objections, than Mrs. Norris interrupted him.

The evasions are given in FIS, though Mrs Norris's arguments in favour of inviting Fanny are given in direct speech. But when, two pages further on, she informs the Bertrams that she herself can take no responsibility and provide no hospitality for Fanny, her words are given in FIS:

> Sir Thomas heard, with some surprise, that it would be totally out of Mrs. Norris's power to take any share in the personal charge of her [Fanny] . . . Mrs. Norris was sorry to say, that the little girl's staying with them, at least as things then were, was quite out of the question. Poor Mr. Norris's indifferent state of health made it an impossibility: he could no more bear the noise of a child than he could fly; if indeed he should ever get well of his gouty complaints, it would be a different matter.

In this latter passage, there is a typical merging of narratorial style into free indirect speech. The first sentence is an instance of what Graham Hough calls 'coloured narrative', since the words 'it would be totally out of Mrs Norris's power' seem to be a quotation of her very words. With 'Mrs Norris was sorry to say' we are in full FIS. In both passages, the use of FIS, while preserving the vivacity of speech and evoking the presence of the speaker, modifies what is said in a subtle, ironical way, if only by juxtaposing the various excuses in a list. As a result, the reader is made keenly aware of the morally indifferent quality, the evasiveness, the selfishness, of what is said, its lack of authenticity.

A not infrequent, non-ironical variation of this function of FIS is its use for a purely formal, conventional exchange of words between Fanny and her sister Susan, about having tea; what is said does not deserve to be given in direct speech (III, 7, 383–4).

FIS is as much used for the reproduction of thoughts as of words; the idiom in which the thoughts are expressed is always close to the normal speech of the character. Particular words are sometimes italicised in the text in order to give the stressed intonation of the speaker or thinker and to make clear the subjective provenance of the statement. Such distinctions are the more necessary because the first person is lost in FIS, and it is sometimes difficult to know whether a 'he' or 'she' refers to the subject or object (sometimes the full name of the subject is repeated, for clarity's sake, even though the sentence emanates from this same person).

When Maria Bertram is vexed at the prospect of her father's early return from the West Indies (I, 11, 107):

> Maria was more to be pitied than Julia [. . .] It was a gloomy prospect, and all that she could do was to throw a mist over it, and hope when the mist cleared away, she should see something else. It would hardly be *early* in November, there were generally delays, a bad passage or *something;* that favouring *something* which every body who shuts their eyes [. . .] feels the comfort of.

The interweaving of narratorial and subjective statement is typical, and in this case the final narratorial comment makes it all the clearer that the earlier sentence presents Maria's thought.

In addition to such typical 'short snatches' of FIS, longer passages also occur. After Fanny has received Henry Crawford's offer of marriage, which he reinforces with the news that he has got her brother a commision in the Navy, Fanny is thrown into great agitation, described in a rather long monologue conducted in FIS (II, 12, 302):

> She was feeling, thinking, trembling, about every thing;—agitated, happy, miserable, infinitely obliged, absolutely angry. It was all beyond belief! He was inexcusable, incomprehensible!—But such were his habits, that he could do nothing

without a mixture of evil. He had previously made her the hap-
piest of human beings, and now he had insulted—she knew not
what to say—how to class or how to regard it. She would not
have him serious, and yet what could excuse the use of such
words and offers, if they meant but to trifle?

But William was a Lieutenant.—*That* was a fact beyond a
doubt.

The FIS continues for a further five lines, and like the few other such
passages, is a true inner monologue. It skilfully presents the whirl and
confusion of thought and feeling in Fanny's mind, and uses the sort of
phrases, the sort of emphases, that would be characteristic of her
speech. But one cannot call them 'her own words', as Hough would
claim, since the reader feels the passage to be reduction made by the
narrator of a multiple confused self-argument whirling in Fanny's
head.

A particularly complex example of FIS presents the speech of one
character as it is sifted through the consciousness of another. Edu-
mund has failed to persuade his brother Tom to drop the theatricals
(their argument is given in direct speech), and then tries his sisters,
Maria and Julia (I, 13, 128–9):

> His sisters, to whom he had an opportunity of speaking the
> next morning, were quite as impatient of his advice [. . .] as
> Tom.—Their mother had no objection to the plan, and they
> were not in the least afraid of their father's disap-
> probation.—There could be no harm in what had been done in
> so many respectable families, and by so many women of the first
> consideration; and it must be scrupulousness run mad, that could
> see anything to censure in a plan like their's, comprehending only
> brothers and sisters, and intimate friends, and which would
> never be heard of beyond themselves. Julia *did* seem inclined to
> admit Maria's situation might require particular caution and
> delicacy—but that could not extend to *her*—*she* was at liberty;
> and Maria evidently considered her engagement as only raising
> her so much above restraint, and leaving her less occasion than
> Julia, to consult either father or mother. Edmund had little to
> hope, but he was still urging the subject, when Henry Crawford
> entered the room, fresh from the Parsonage, calling out, 'No
> want of hands in our Theatre, Miss Bertram'.

In the framework of the narratorial description of Edmund's campaign of persuasion, the arguments of the sisters are given in FIS, to which an abrupt end is put by Henry's intervention, given in direct speech. What is particularly interesting is not only the brilliant evocation of the manner in which the girls argue and speak, but the suggestions that what we are reading is Edmund's registration of what they say. The italicised 'did' and 'she' of Julia's argument, the 'evidently' of Maria's, evoke not only the egoistic girls but also the listener, who is making his cautious and prudent conclusions. We feel in this passage that it is not so much a narrator who is reporting, in FIS, the sisters' arguments, but Edmund himself, who is sifting and arranging them, in order to be able to cope with them. The italicised words bear Julia's emphases in the first place, no doubt, but do they not bear a secondary accent, that of Edmund, just as the word 'evidently' is an interposition by Edmund?

It is not only in this fusion of perspectives that, in such passages, FIS shows itself to be an instrument of meanings that cannot be communicated by other narrative forms. Throughout the book Edmund is so loyal and good a son and brother that he never allows himself criticism of his parents and sisters, and sometimes we are tempted to believe that propriety dulls his intelligence. But here, in the report of his argument with his sisters, we observe irony, understanding of their frivolous and selfish characters, and we can infer throughout the novel that he knows much more than his words, his explicit thoughts, or his behaviour inform us of.

We find in Jane Austen's use of FIS many of the indicators and signals that Bally and Lips were to draw attention to——in the above passage, for instance, the exclamatory question, the characteristic intonation, and characteristic expressions. In general, obtrusive signals like exclamations are less prominent than in many nineteenth-century authors, who like Goethe seem particularly to need them to effect the transition from narratorial style to free indirect. Nor does Jane Austen use a highly characteristic idiom to distinguish the subjective source of a FIS passage. Her own authorial style is very close to that of her characters. It is this closeness, I believe, that facilitates the great mobility of her style, that easy slipping in and out of the different modes of speech, that led Graham Hough to invent the term 'coloured narrative' for prose in which the voice and tone of a character may appear for a moment in the midst of narratorial passages, giving them continually that extra dimension that is such an enrichment and a delight. It also offers many opportunities for the narrator's ironical tone, that modulates the voice of the character. Intricate effects are produced that may actually be misleading for the inattentive reader. In the following passage the shifts of perspective are almost too kaleidoscopic to be followed. When the Crawfords come to stay with the Grants, the description of their feelings about the visit is given in objective narrative that is broken by many phrases that are, as it were, quotations from the character, though fitted into the grammar of narratorial style. These pseudo-quotations I have printed in bold type; in two cases the author herself puts words into italics in order to give a character's emphases (I, 5, 47):

> The Crawfords [. . .] were very willing to stay. Mary was satisfied with the parsonage as a present home, and Henry equally ready to lengthen his visit. He had come, intending to spend only a few days with them, but **Mansfield promised well,** and there was nothing to call him elsewhere. It **delighted** Mrs. Grant to keep them both with her, and Dr. Grant was **exceedingly well contented** to have it so; **a talking pretty young woman** like Miss Crawford, is always pleasant society to an indolent, stay-at-home man; and Mr. Crawford's being his guest was an excuse for drinking claret every day.
>
> The Miss Bertrams' admiration of Mr. Crawford was more **rapturous** than any thing which Miss Crawford's habits made her likely to feel. She acknowledged, however, that the Mr Bertrams were **very fine young men,** that two such young men were not often seen together even in London, and that their manners, particularly those of the eldest, were very good. *He* had been much in London, and had more **liveliness and gallantry** than Edmund, and **must, therefore, be preferred;** and, indeed, his being the eldest was another strong claim. She had **felt an early presentiment** that she *should* **like the eldest best.** She knew **it was her way.**

There is here hardly a completed sentence in FIS; the device appears only in odd phrases scattered about, some of which bear the unmistakeable tang of the character concerned. Most of these 'quotations' are both characteristic and ironical, the set attributed to Mary Crawford, for instance, displaying her sophistication, near-cynicism, and sharp self-knowledge. But the narratorial style runs throughout, framing the FIS, and in it there is explicit irony too, like the comment on the 'excuse for drinking claret'. It would be pedantic to criticise so sparkling a piece, but it is not easy to keep up with the repeated switches, and easy to mistake the subtle irony clinging to the

FIS statements for a rather crude narratorial irony. Such confusions are most likely to be avoided by reading the passage aloud, when the mimicry wins its full force.

The passage offers valuable testimony as to the origins of free indirect speech. One can imagine Jane Austen speaking to a sister or niece about their acquaintance in just this mixture of personal opinion and incidental minicry, and can believe that the source of the literary device lay in actual usage.

An additional interest arises in respect to the narratorial perspective. While for the central characters, Fanny and Edmund, those most sympathetic to the narrator, free indirect speech is often used to reproduce their thoughts and feelings, their unspoken reflections, the same free access to hidden mental processes is not available in the case of the other characters, such as the Crawfords and the Grants, and even Edmund's brother and sisters. Here, as we quickly observe, their thoughts are constructed out of the words they might, or do characteristically use; in fact, free indirect speech as used for them largely reproduces what they actually say. The narrator's insight seems therefore, in their regard, to be based upon the sort of evidence that would be available to a bystander (albeit a somewhat ubiquitous one), that is, upon the character's behaviour and expressions. It is as if the beam of the narrator's attention is focused sharply on Fanny, less brightly on Edmund, while the other characters are placed in the penumbra at varying distances from the centre, the distance being inversely proportionate to their role in the story and the sympathy they are allowed to claim. We can admire the sureness with which this narratorial stance and perspective are maintained. But it also demonstrates how inadequate is the term 'omniscient narrator' for this type of narrative, since, while omniscience can properly denote the narrator's relation to Fanny, the whole structure of the story and its impact on the reader depends on the varying distribution of knowledge and intimacy in respect to the other characters.

The effect of free indirect speech is, of course, something the reader perceives intuitively. In many cases it is difficult theoretically to unravel its operation, especially since various effects are present simultaneously. Complications occur particularly when FIS alternates in short snatches with narratorial account and direct speech, and I believe that at times the subjective implications of FIS spill over into the neighbouring types of statement. Such a 'contamination', as Bally called it, may be of considerable importance in the interpretation of a work, and my last example is intended to be a contribution to one of the most troublesome questions that arise from *Mansfield Park:* what is Fanny's true attitude to Lady Bertram, the benefactress to whom she is so much more loyal and devoted than to her own mother? Does Fanny allow herself to notice that Lady Bertram, good-natured as she is, is indolent, easy-going, and selfish? The narrator leaves the reader in no doubt on the fact; but does Fanny know it?

When the eldest Bertram, Tom, falls dangerously ill, Fanny is away from Mansfield Park on a visit to her mother, so that she hears about it only in letters from Lady Bertram. Fanny is distressed and most anxious to help, though she also cannot repress her own private anxiety about a feared reconciliation between Edmund and Mary Crawford. After the first letter from Lady Bertram we read (III, 13, 427):

> Fanny's feelings on the occasion were indeed considerably more warm and genuine than her aunt's style of writing. She felt truly for them all. Tom dangerously ill, Edmund gone to attend him, and the sadly small party remaining at Mansfield, were cares to shut out every other care, or almost every other. She could just find selfishness enough to wonder whether Edmund *had* written to Miss Crawford before this summons came, but no sentiment dwelt long with her, that was not purely affectionate and disinterestedly anxious. Her aunt did not neglect her; she wrote again and again; they were receiving frequent accounts from Edmund, and these accounts were as regularly transmitted to Fanny, in the same diffuse style, and the same medley of trusts, hopes, and fears, all following and producing each other at hap-hazard. It was a sort of playing at being frightened.

There can be no doubt that the sentences beginning 'Tom dangerously ill' and 'She could just find selfishness enough' are FIS—only Fanny could call her concern over Edmund 'selfish'—though the second half of this sentence is narratorial. There can also be no doubt that much is narratorial, like the second half of the second FIS sentence, and especially the comments on the 'diffuse style', the 'medley of trusts, hopes, and fears', in Lady Bertram's letters, and the sharp last sentence. When we analyse the passage, we can sufficiently clearly distinguish between objective, narratorial statements and subjective, and can see that decisive criticism of Lady Bertram is allowed only to the narrator. But the effect of the juxtaposition and mingling of the two stylistic modes is very complex, and it is difficult to read the passage without transferring some of the dispassionate clarity of the narrator to Fanny, who reads and ponders the letters, who tries to unravel the information, and must often sigh with disappointment at their confusion and triviality. I believe we may conclude that, while Fanny accepts fully the obligations of respect and affection with regard to her benefactress, we are meant to understand that she is not blinded by propriety (or self-interest), but observes with clear perception. When Jane Austen remarked that Fanny was morally better than her author, I think she did not mean her to be obtuse. Sharp critics of Fanny's moral character will not think her awareness makes her character any better.

It is astonishing that so rich and sure a use of free indirect speech is to be found in Jane Austen's novels, when she had so slight a tradition to build on. That she could so unforcedly exploit so many potentialities of the device is, no doubt, in part due to the whole artistic intention of her work, her profound concern for the changing patterns of personal relationships within a small socio-cultural group, small enough and sufficiently distant from great issues and events to permit intimacy and encourage attention to nuances. This stylistic form of free indirect speech corresponded to the moral and narrative structure of the novels. By no means all the resources of the style are used. Most notably lacking are two features that later became prominent. First, while FIS in Jane Austen's works reproduces or evokes the words or thoughts of characters, it is not used to evoke the physical scene, the manner in which the characters are aware of the landscape, the house or room, the physical appearance of other people, and similar visual and auditory phenomena. There is of course extremely little description of external appearances and scenes in narratorial form too, and hardly a trace, I believe, in FIS. Second, the responses that appear in FIS are nearly all such as can properly be called thoughts, i.e. such as can be articulated in words and grammatical sentences. Agitation, confusion of mind, may be evoked by broken or incomplete sentences, but verbalisation, rationalisation, remains firm in spite of such vacillation. It was to be a long time before writers found out how to render inner movements, perceptions, reactions at the levels that precede thought and words, before they have found the way to consciousness and articulate utterance. To some extent these two features lacking in Jane Austen's novels are allied, for both indicate that area of nervous, sentient, emotional reaction that precedes or eludes verbalisation. Perhaps one should say that the absence of this sort of response is due to a profound distrust on Jane Austen's part, for these non-rational responses do not simply precede consciousness, they may resist or even challenge rationality and consciousness. The discovery of how stylistically to express them belongs to a positive valuation of them that Jane Austen did not share.

Georg Büchner: *Lenz*

The last of these early fictional works to be included here, Georg Büchner's Novelle *Lenz* (1836), is of a very different character from the novels of Goethe or Jane Austen. It is associated with them here because in them all free indirect speech is a substantive element in the structure of the works, not occasional or incidental. But *Lenz* offers little in the way of reproduction of the words or articulate thoughts of characters that can be compared with that in the extensive novel. Brief as it is, however, it discovers another and vast potentiality of free indirect speech.

It is an account of the mental breakdown of the poet Lenz in the winter 1777–8, in a district—Alsace—where Büchner himself was a proscribed refugee from Hesse. Based on a diary-like record by the clergyman J. F. Oberlin, to whom Lenz had gone in search of shelter and spiritual help, Büchner's story has something of the quality of a diary, though strangely transformed. The events of these three winter weeks are described by an impersonal narrator, who aligns himself closely with Lenz's own perspective, in that he confines himself to the field of experience of his central character, and explains no more about persons than Lenz knows, or in some cases tells us little because for Lenz himself the information is superfluous—for instance, who his friend Kaufmann is or who is the girl who obsesses his memory. But also, from time to time the narrator detaches himself from Lenz, perhaps to describe his appearance, his childish face lit up by the lamp in the circle of the Oberlin household, perhaps to discuss his mental state, when he suggests that Lenz's suicidal impulses were essentially, like his self-infliction of physical pain, a means to shock himself out of panic fears and delusions. The narrator is also prominent in the sense that there is an abundance of explicit reporting, with verbs like 'he said', 'he thought', 'he was of opinion'. There are even two occasions when the narrator assumes the historian's or editor's mantle, to tell us of a similar event in the life of a contemporary of Lenz, or to introduce Lenz's ideas on art with the information that this was the time when 'the idealistic period was beginning'.

There is therefore a firmly objective narratorial framework to Büchner's story. Most of the conversation and articulate thought is given either in direct speech or in indirect governed by 'he said' or 'he thought'. Only occasionally is free indirect speech used for this purpose, the most notable case occurring when, as Lenz's religious faith weakens, he remembers earlier experiences of religious exaltation and despairs over his present apathy:

> Memories came to him of the times when a turmoil seethed in him, when he panted under the pressure of his feelings. And now so dead! He despaired of himself; then he threw himself down, he wrung his hands, he stirred up everything in himself—but dead! dead! Then he implored God to send him a sign.

> Es kamen ihm Erinnerungen an die Zeiten, wo alles in sich drängte, wo er unter all seinen Empfindungen keuchte. Und jetzt so tot! Er verzweifelte an sich selbst; dann warf er sich nieder, er rang die Hände, er rührte alles in sich auf—aber tot! tot! Dann flehte er, Gott möge ein Zeichen an ihm tun.

The exclamations are typical FIS, interrupting momentarily the narrative flow.

A more complex example of changing perspective is given in the report of Lenz's views on art, as he expounds them in conversation with Kaufmann:

> He said: the poets who are said to give reality also had no inkling of it; yet they were, at any rate, more bearable than those who wanted to transfigure reality. He said: Our dear Lord has after all made the world as it was meant to be, and we can't botch together anything better; our one endeavour must be, to create a little in imitation of Him. I demand in everything—Life, the possibility of existing, and that's enough; we do not have to proceed to ask whether it is beautiful, whether it is ugly. The feeling that what has been created has life stands above these two and is the only criterion in art.

> Er sagte: Die Dichter, von denen man sage, sie geben die Wirklichkeit, hätten auch keine Ahnung davon; doch seien sie immer noch erträglicher als die, welche die Wirklichkeit verklären wollten. Er sagte: Der liebe Gott hat die Welt wohl gemacht, wie sie sein soll, und wir können wohl nicht was Besseres klecksen; unser einziges Bestreben soll sein, ihm ein wenig nachzuschaffen. Ich verlange in allem—Leben, Möglichkeit des Daseins, und dann ist's gut; wir haben dann

nicht zu fragen, ob es schön, ob es hässlich ist. Das Gefühl, dass was geschaffen sei Leben habe, stehe über diesen beiden und sei das einzige Kriterium in Kunstsachen.

The account of his views continues, and is clearly not the report of one speech but of a number of his observations in the course of a discussion. It is somewhat difficult to analyse from the translation since the functioning of the subjunctive in the German cannot be reproduced in English. What Lenz says is first given in indirect speech with the subjunctive, which implicitly asserts 'this is what he actually said'. This mood is then replaced by the indicative, with the emergence of the first person, 'we' or 'I'. It returns then to the indirect with the subjunctive, and this alternation continues until Lenz recounts a personal experience in the indicative past, and sums up his doctrine in generalisations all in the present indicative; this last part is indistinguishable from direct speech. The reader will not consciously register these changes of mood and tense; what he will feel is a variation in the intensity of feeling and thought in Lenz, a warmth and conviction in his voice when the indicative and first person are used. There is no free indirect speech here. The narrator reduces himself, whether using indirect or direct speech, to the bare role of a reporter, whose modest factuality here and elsewhere (as Büchner might have learned from Oberlin's account) gives Lenz's vivacity, suffering, and desolation an extraordinary poignancy.

In other parts of the work, this reticence of the narrator takes a quite different form; through free indirect speech he repeatedly enriches his own account with Lenz's own perspective, and the mingling of the two perspectives is often so intimate that we can speak of a dual voice. This is the most remarkable innovation of this Novelle. It does not affect actual speech, nor does it reproduce what normally would be considered to be thoughts. This style is very marked in the opening paragraphs of the Novelle, though it recurs on several occasions, all passages of description.[33] We can perhaps best examine it in the opening sentences of the work:

> On the 20th of January Lenz crossed the mountains. The peaks and high slopes in snow, down the valleys grey stones, green patches, cliffs and firs. It was wet and cold; the water trickled down the rocks and leapt over the path. The branches of the firs sagged heavily in the damp air. Grey clouds drove over the sky, but all so dense—and then the mist came steaming up

and drifted heavy and damp through the bushes, so sluggish, so clumsy.

Den 20 (Jänner) ging Lenz durchs Gebirg. Die Gipfel und hohen Bergflächen im Schnee, die Täler hinunter graues Gestein, grüne Flächen, Felsen und Tannen. Es war nasskalt; das Wasser rieselte die Felsen hinunter und sprang über den Weg. Die Äste der Tannen hingen schwer herab in die feuchte Luft. Am Himmel zogen graue Wolken, aber alles so dicht—und dann dampfte der Nebel herauf und strich schwer und feucht durch das Gesträuch, so träg, so plump.

A simple narratorial statement opens, to be followed by many such later. A schedule of items follows, brief and without verbs like a memorandum, that seems at first sight to belong to this objective narrator. But 'down the valleys' ('die Täler hinunter') administers a first shock. For this does not say 'down in the valleys', an objective siting, and the 'hin' tells us the narrator is standing beside Lenz, looking 'down into the valleys'. As we become aware of this, we begin to feel that the itemising of the landscape expresses not so much an authorial mode as Lenz's situation, his nervous and restless distractedness, that cannot dwell for long on anything. The next sentence is securely objective and factual like the first, but the following has the curious accusative of 'hingen [. . .] in die feuchte Luft', literally 'hung [. . .] into the damp air'. There is in this a slightly uncanny suggestion, perhaps of a voluntary movement, which we can only feel emanates from some irrational apprehension in Lenz. While the following 'grey clouds drove over the sky' is objective, the exclamatory 'so dense' is subjective, a gasp of fear that brings the lurking panic in Lenz's mind into the open (it is not certain whether 'dicht' here means 'dense' or 'close'). Several other elements in this last sentence reinforce the subjective impact. 'And then' is a term that signals a succession of events, but the movement of the mist does not succeed another event, and the term indicates that dislocation in Lenz's thinking that later paragraphs make still more explicit. 'Up' ('herauf') again puts us in Lenz's physical position, with the mist swirling up towards him, and the final exclamations 'so sluggish, so clumsy' not only assert this phrase to be free indirect speech, but are words that only a man in his strained and endangered mental state would use, for the application to the mist of terms that are essentially human again suggests the nearness to panic.

In the next short paragraph, not quoted above, which is entirely in objective form, we are told that the journey did not tire Lenz but that 'he sometimes felt it to be unpleasant that he could not walk on his head'. The unemphatic matter-of-fact comment again shows the narrator assimilating Lenz's own acceptance of his wish as normal.

In the great paragraph that follows, which describes the violent storm over the mountains, with Lenz's imaginations, delusions, his exaltation and panic, his reconquest of serenity and clear vision, we are never allowed completely to lose the guidance of the narrator, whose presence is continually asserted through simple descriptive statements and comments. He tells us, for instance, that Lenz constantly miscalculated distances; he uses many similes when describing the storm, thus indicating a distance between what the storm was and what it seemed like to Lenz. But at the same time we constantly accompany Lenz, experience his fantasies, panics, and temporary serenity. The structure of the sentences, some of them gigantic, breathless, changing direction both in content and syntax, changing speed, piled with images, itself communicates Lenz's experience direct. We feel the similes are his, not the narrator's. Though the style is, on the surface, mainly simple indirect speech, governed by such indications as 'it seemed to him', 'he did not understand', 'he thought', within this reported speech there grows a peculiar form of free indirect speech, so that the narratorial description communicates itself as Lenz's own, actual experience of the storm, using his own terms. Very unobtrusive stylistic idiosyncracies contribute to this effect. In the narratorial description of the storm there is an unusually large number of impersonal constructions, based on normal usage with regard to the weather, but here so used that they transmit to the reader Lenz's feeling that the violent processes in nature, and in his own emotions, are the product of mighty, unknowable, and uncontrollable forces. The frequent use of the undefined pronoun 'all' in place of a more concrete term also reveals that perilous vagueness in his understanding and his longings, that alternates with abnormal vividness of perception and insight.

It would need the whole great paragraph to demonstrate the complexity of this effect, and I must be content with two brief examples:

Only at times, when the storm hurled the clouds into the valleys and they came steaming up through the forest, and the voices awoke against the cliffs [. . .]

Nur manchmal, wenn der Sturm das Gewölk in die Täler warf

und es den Wald herauf dampfte, und die Stimmen an den Felsen
wach wurden [. . .]

'Came up' ('herauf') establishes the subjective perspective, but the
most interesting element is the 'voices'. We are not told what or whose
voices, we can understand that they are formed as echoes against the
cliff-faces. But we do not enquire about them, because we have
adopted Lenz's standpoint, and the voices are as natural, as un-
questionable, to us readers as they are to him.

So also, as the day closes and the storm abates, when Lenz stands at
the height of the pass and looks over the panorama of peaks:

> Towards evening it had grown quieter; the cloud-bank lay firm
> and motionless in the sky; as far as the eye could reach, nothing
> but peaks, from which broad slopes of snow led downward, and
> all so still, grey, dusky. He felt appallingly lonely; he was alone,
> utterly alone.

> Es war gegen Abend ruhiger geworden; das Gewölk lag fest und
> unbeweglich am Himmel; soweit der Blick reichte, nichts als
> Gipfel, von denen sich breite Flächen hinabzogen, und alles so
> still, grau, dämmernd. Es wurde ihm entsetzlich einsam; er war
> allein, ganz allein.

The opening might well be narratorial, but as soon as the view is
described, we are placed beside Lenz. The exclamatory 'so still, grey,
dusky' confirms this. The expression 'nothing but peaks' seems
perhaps odd at first until we recognise it as free indirect speech, as
Lenz's response, that betrays an irrational irritation in his mind.
Similarly, the last phrase 'he was alone, utterly alone' would be
bathetic if it were the narrator's; as free indirect speech it reveals
Lenz's despairing awareness of his perilous isolation (I suppose it is
sheer chance that exactly the same switch to free indirect speech with
'He was alone' occurs at the end of J.-P. Sartre's *The Age of Reason*).

In a few cases, in these paragraphs, free indirect speech expresses a
thought of the character. But such thoughts are scarcely articulated,
formulated, and do not form a logical sequence. They are more in the
nature of isolated words like 'alone', or of vague feelings, like Lenz's
wish to merge with the universe. Mostly, however, his mental activity
expresses itself through the formation of images, what he sees and
hears is interpreted through metaphors and similes, sometimes more
rational, sometimes more hallucinatory. The strain and tension in his
mind is also expressed, as I have said, through the syntax of long

sentences, in which the storm evokes complex associations of images. What Büchner discovers in free indirect speech is not the reproduction of thoughts so much as that of the most immediate responses to experience, the first nervous reactions, the spontaneous and uncontrolled images, the inchoate and floating words that precede what we would normally call consciousness, namely, the state in which we can formulate an experience or idea in articulated sentences which can be communicated to others. It is of course no accident that the medium through whom Büchner could achieve this, Lenz, was a man of vivid imagination and acute sensitivity, accustomed to the literary use and combination of images, undergoing a crisis of mental dislocation (the Novelle ends with Lenz's complete breakdown in utter apathy).

The great limitation of Büchner's achievement is that only one character can thus be known. The narrator so identifies himself with the main character that other characters acquire no substance; they and the whole environment exist for us only through Lenz's mind. The work is indeed highly lyrical in character, presenting like a lyric both the direct experience of the subject and through its form the distancing reflection of the author. There is good reason for its being so short. We can scarcely imagine the method being carried on for long. The distinctive achievement of the work depends on the fact that the central character is in a state of heightened awareness, on the edge of derangement and apathy, yet because of this all the more acutely observant and responsive and imaginatively creative, so that the world he sees, and that is transmitted to us, is brilliant and unique. But it is only *his* world. No other characters communicate their view, their perspective, their reality. If the Novelle had been continued in the same style, it might have become wearisome, or a study in neurotic obsession. As it is, it has the intensity of a lyric, and is somewhat lacking both in the epic and the dramatic quality of the novel. It was to be the affair of others, above all of Dostoyevsky, to embody this lyrical element within the organism of epic narrative.

VI

Victorians

Dickens and mimicry: *Bleak House*

There are few cases of free indirect speech to be found in Walter Scott's novels. The two examples from *The Heart of Mid-Lothian* quoted earlier show that its absence is not due to inability to handle the form or recognise where it might be appropriate. It would seem more likely that the author has so much of a tale to tell, in which the striking incidents must be ordered in clear outlines and proportions, that the author's guiding hand needs to remain firmly in control, in respect to both the events and the moral judgement attending them. Such FIS as there is, for instance in *The Antiquary,* is very occasional and does not bear great significance. Very much the same is true for Balzac and Stendhal; in both, the tense and varied action requires a prominent narrator, whose imaginative sweep bears the story along and controls it. In these authors, it is true, the characters themselves, complex, impassioned, and often highly self-conscious, can claim a central significance for their specific view-point; in Scott, the characters are generally too limited in insight, passion, and intellectual scope to be adequate voices of experience; even landscape descriptions require the authorial voice. In Balzac and Stendhal, however, there is much reflection by the characters, and though this is usually expressed in the direct spoken-monologue form, one feels at times that in them the FIS that Flaubert was soon to make familiar is on the point of breaking out. Yet their rich, extravagant imaginations cannot, like Flaubert's, subject themselves to the characters they create. And one might say of Dickens, too, that his imagination cannot brook a rival; he, not a character, has to be the medium of description if all potentialities are to be uncovered. Perhaps it was this extravagant, almost riotously rich character of his imagination that induced him to invent a personal narrator for some of his novels and thus impose some discipline on his fantasy (even though his invented narrators may on occasion overstep their limits).

At this point, something may be said regarding the relationship of the first-person narrative to FIS. The examples so far examined show

FIS as a function of a narrator who, unnameable and non-personal, has the right of access to the inner world of the characters. It can rarely be appropriate to a personalised narrator since, once his personality is defined, his range of insight is reduced to that of a real person. Authors often try to profit from the authenticity that the invention of a personalised narrator gives, without observing the limitations it imposes. *Madame Bovary* and *The Brothers Karamazov*, for instance, both begin as the narratives of a specific narrator-person, who is soon utterly discarded by Flaubert and only occasionally resuscitated by Dostoyevsky, for essential aspects of both novels contradict the character of a personal narrative. This contradiction does not disturb us greatly, or at all, where the invented narrator is so faintly sketched in as in these great novels, and in particular where he is not actually engaged as a participant in the story, but is a mere onlooker.

But when we speak of Dickens's first-person novels, *David Copperfield* or *Great Expectations,* we mean a type of novel in which the narrator is not only personalised, but also is the most prominent participant in the story. In this type, it is impossible to attribute to the narrator the power of knowing the unexpressed thoughts of another character than himself, without distorting the central character, the narrator, himself. He may, of course, suggest and guess what they might be, but must always make it clear that such observations are only inferences. The narrative form he uses postulates distance between himself and the other characters. Thus the chief source of free indirect speech is closed to him. The narrator can evoke through FIS what he himself is experiencing and has experienced at an earlier time; he can also use FIS for reporting the actual speech of characters. In this last case the subtle modulations that can be introduced through the narratorial voice and tone, for instance the irony so often evident, make its use somewhat perilous, unless the narrator is intended to be fairly sophisticated. FIS therefore, though not absent from first-person novels, is comparatively rare, and sometimes contrary to the very spirit of the story. This is the case, too, with epistolary novels.

Bleak House (1852–3) gives the opportunity of examining both the main narrative forms, since some parts of the novel are told in the first person as 'Esther's narrative', while the rest, in the third person, transmits the authoritative, objective account of an impersonal, or rather non-personal narrator. Our discussion is complicated by the fact that these third-person sections are throughout composed in the present tense (the 'historic present'), so that the tense of the indirect, reported speech is also the present. 'Esther's narrative' is however told in the normal past tense.

The two alternating narrative modes of *Bleak House*, the narratorial and the first-person accounts, constitute contrasting modes of feeling and blocks of experience. In its material and style, Esther's narrative defines a sheltered security—psychological, social, and moral—that, though not immune from dangers and sometimes brought into contact with disasters, is itself unassailable. It is necessarily a retrospective account, which formally implies the security of a standpoint that at least implies survival, and explicitly promises a final happy outcome. In the third-person authorial sections we are immersed in the terrors and evil of life, the pullulating London world with its unfathomable and uncontrollable catastrophes, its background of passion and greed, depicted with the emotional involvement and grotesque fantasy commensurate with so lawless and terrifying a world. The narrator's voice is not that of a person, it seems to be the voice of the events themselves, and it lacks all the reassuring comfort that a personal voice might transmit. In both narrative forms, free indirect speech is rare and brief.

In the narratorial sections FIS is almost always used for humorous–satirical purposes, and often seems to be an enlarged version of those fixed catch-phrases through which many of Dickens's characters define themselves; for instance, with 'Certainly, Jo don't know' the narrator answers in Jo's own words and grammar a question he himself has put (chapter 16, p. 220).[34] This type of FIS is near the common usage in ordinary conversational speech, as we have seen it in more refined versions in Jane Austen's novels. More complex is the use of FIS within the framework of a conversation otherwise carried on in direct speech (again there are examples in Jane Austen).

Lady Dedlock, already aware of the baneful suspicions of Tulkinghorn, the solicitor, wishes to speak to her husband, and goes to the library where she expects to find him alone; as she begins to speak, she notices that Tulkinghorn is with him (48, p. 653):

'Sir Leicester, I am desirous—but you are engaged.'

O dear no! Not at all. Only Mr. Tulkinghorn.

Always at hand. Haunting every place. No relief or security from him for a moment.

'I beg your pardon, Lady Dedlock. Will you allow me to retire?'

With a look that plainly says, 'You know you have the power to remain if you will,' she tells him it is not necessary, and moves towards a chair.

The direct speech of Lady Dedlock's entrance is answered by phrases of her husband's that are not enclosed in inverted commas, though it might seem that they are in fact direct speech. Then her mental response to Tulkinghorn's presence, spasmodic, not spoken, is given in FIS, evoking the terror under which she lives. Tulkinghorn's smooth politeness, in direct speech, re-establishes the linguistic controls of normalcy. Though Sir Leicester's answer, upon her entrance, contains none of the distinctive signs of FIS, it might be counted as such; but before discussing its effect, let us consider similar situations.

When, in the midst of a conversation between Lady Dedlock and the clerk Guppy, the latter tells her he can 'produce' the boy Jo at any time, her answer comes in FIS: 'The wretched boy is nothing to my Lady, and she does *not* wish to have him produced' (29, 408). The effect of the indirect form here is clear. Throughout this encounter Lady Dedlock is fending off Guppy's insinuations and onslaught, hiding her anxiety under the mask of her social superiority. With this answer Guppy comes up against the blank wall of her aristocratic hauteur. The words she uses are not important; we hear only the 'wretched boy', the contemptuous 'produced', and the stressed 'not'. All that is important is the rebuff she administers and that Guppy is conscious of. The same device is adopted in the friendly exchange between Trooper George and Mr Woodcourt, when they are joining forces to help poor Jo. George asks Mr Woodcourt whether he knows Esther and whether he is related to her, and the answer in both cases is given in indirect form: 'Yes, it appears', 'No, it appears' (47, 642). It is clear on this occasion that the answer is given as it is registered by the listener, George; in so delicate a personal matter Woodcourt withdraws into taciturn middle-class formalism and the Trooper is gently but firmly rebuffed.

Sir Leicester's answer to his wife is in form similar to these. Common to them all is the transference of emphasis and attention from what is said to its effect on the listener. The reader only 'gathers' what is said, but is aware at the same time of the response of the listener; the statements are therefore free indirect speech as formulated in the consciousness of the listener, and evoke his response to the utterance. In the case of Sir Leicester's answer, the indirect form is of course not connected with any social rebuff. Here it merely emphasises the formal, inane character of the statement, its banality, which contrasts so painfully for Lady Dedlock with the dire threat of Tulkinghorn's presence.

When Esther uses this form in her narrative, the same effect is achieved. She meets Woodcourt on his return from India, and asks him, a doctor, about the health of her friend Richard (45, 625): ' "You do not think he is ill?" I said. No. He looked robust in body.' The only sign that the answer is indirect speech is the tense of 'looked', which is in the past in order to conform with an unwritten 'He said that . . .'. We readily understand that the form indicates that Esther is concerned with the assurance in the reply, not the particular words. Put thus, in the form of free indirect speech, the words seem also to bear a greater assurance than direct speech would, since the latter would be more clearly only the words of Woodcourt. Free indirect speech does, in certain cases, seem to reinforce the opinion of a character with the narrator's authority. Here, it transmits in this way Esther's authority, but with delicate irony revealing her wish to quieten her apprehensions.

The subtlety of function in these simple examples shows how flexible FIS is, how responsive to its context.

On some occasions Dickens uses the deictic particles of time—'tonight', 'last night', 'next day', etc.—that place the reader in the time-situation of the character, and hence provoke FIS. Though these particles and phrases are sometimes used rather loosely, without differentiation between 'next day' and 'the next day', between 'last night' and 'the night before' etc., he usually does clearly distinguish 'yesterday' from 'the day before', 'this afternoon' from 'that afternoon', 'today' from 'that day', and so forth; that is, he distinguishes the subjective from the objective use. We even find Esther's narrative using the form that conjures up the subjective present (4, 34): 'A carriage would be at Mrs Jellyby's [...] early in the forenoon of to-morrow'. The 'to-morrow' is more sprightly and imaginative than we would expect in Esther's rather demure narrative, but in this context it properly enhances the longing for the morrow to arrive.

Such adverbs are used more appropriately in the third-person, authorial sections of the novel. In chapter 25 Mrs Snagsby's obsessive suspicions of her husband lead her to imagine some collusion between him and Jo, so that the fate of the boy can be described, at this point, through her eyes. The fairly long passage of FIS includes the deictic 'yesterday', 'to-morrow night', and 'here' (25, 356):

> But happily (and Mrs. Snagsby tightly shakes her head and tightly smiles), that boy was met by Mr. Chadband yesterday in the streets; and that boy [. . .] was seized by Mr. Chadband and threatened with being delivered over to the police, unless he

showed the reverend gentleman where he lived, and unless he entered into, and fulfilled, an undertaking to appear in Cook's Court to-morrow night—'to-mor-row-night', Mrs. Snagsby repeats for mere emphasis, with another tight smile, and another tight shake of her head; and to-morrow night that boy will be here, and to-morrow night Mrs. Snagsby will have her eye upon him and upon some one else; and O you may walk a long while in your secret ways (says Mrs. Snagsby with haughtiness and scorn), but you can't blind ME!

The occurrences of the day before are recalled by Mrs Snagsby, and reproduced in FIS, which is twice interrupted by direct speech, first the 'to-morrow night' addressed to Jo, later the triumphant warning directed at her husband that is clearly not spoken but shaped in her mind. The brilliant passage demonstrates how FIS can add a dimension to narrative, since we experience simultaneously both the cruel hectoring of Jo and the mental attitude, the tone and gesture, of the tormentors.

One of the characteristic features of Dickens's style is the use of the personal idiom of the characters, which is also very often the idiom of a group, especially of the common people, the illiterate. Such phrases are often woven into the narrative, sometimes singled out by inverted commas. Thus, in chapter 11 of *Bleak House,* we are told that the estrangement between Mrs Perkins and Mrs Piper is a consequence of 'young Perkins having "fetched" young Piper "a crack" '. Very many of the FIS passages are extensions of this type of quotation of personal idiom, from which the normal narratorial grammatical framework and the inverted commas have been removed. There are particularly many examples in this chapter, which describes the coroner's court investigating the death of Mr Nemo.

A simple example occurs just before the post-mortem, when a crowd of youths are chanting taunts at the beadle (11, 144):

> Policeman at last finds it necessary to support the law, and seize a vocalist; who is released upon the flight of the rest, on condition of his getting out of this then, come! and cutting it—a condition he immediately observes.

The policeman's words, with the deictic 'this', the exclamatory 'come!', and the typical slang 'cutting it', are clearly direct speech. One can hardly call this free indirect speech, its syntax is even more audacious.

This audacity is ordered, at a further stage, into free indirect speech, in the account of Mrs Piper's evidence (p. 147). The narrator interrupts the account to tell us she uses the word 'plaintive' for the deceased, and we can see that from time to time the coroner checks her with a question that is not reported:

> Why, Mrs. Piper has a good deal to say, chiefly in parentheses and without punctuation, but not much to tell. Mrs. Piper lives in the court (which her husband is a cabinet-maker), and it has long been well beknown among her neighbours [. . .] as the Plaintive—so Mrs. Piper insists on calling the deceased—was reported to have sold himself. Thinks it was the Plaintive's air in which that report originatinin. See the Plaintive often and considered as his air was feariocious and not to be allowed to go about some children being timid [. . .] Has seen the Plaintive wexed and worrited by the children [. . .] On accounts of this and his dark looks has often dreamed as she see him take a pick-axe from his pocket and split Johnny's head (which child knows not fear and has repeatedly called after him close at his eels).

It is a marvellous piece of rambling inconsequence, but the grammatical form of this shapeless statement is precise and shapely, the form of free indirect speech. The use of the present tense for the narrative disguises this, since verbs like 'has seen', 'has dreamed' reproduce the tense Mrs Piper actually uses in her testimony. While the present tense, therefore, invites us to take her statement as direct speech, with all its personal idiom and grammar, this is misleading, since it is used only because the introductory narrative verbs are in the present; the use of the third person for the speaker indicates decisively that it is all free indirect speech. In the first place, one is tempted to say, it makes the impact of direct speech, evoking so vividly the person and words of Mrs Piper. In fact, however, it also bears the stamp of the narrator, for in the form of indirect speech the humour is more concentrated, even more fantastic, than it would be in direct speech. One may even suspect the narrator of parody here and there; for example it is difficult to imagine the context in which Mrs Piper would refer to 'which my husband', and here the narrator seems to be imitating her style. I think it right to call this exuberantly gay passage humorous, with an undertone of affection, rather than satirical or ironic.

This passage is followed by the appearance at court of Jo, who is to give evidence, and here again we observe a transition from an audacious mixture of direct and narratorial account to free indirect speech:

> Says the Coroner, is that boy here? Says the beadle, no, sir, he is not here. Says the Coroner, go and fetch him then. In the absence of the active and intelligent [beadle], the Coroner converses with Mr. Tulkinghorn.
>
> O! Here's the boy, gentlemen!
>
> Here he is, very muddy, very hoarse, very ragged. Now, boy!—But stop a minute. Caution. This boy must be put through a few preliminary paces.
>
> Name, Jo. Nothing else that he knows on. Don't know that everybody has two names. Never heerd of sich a think. Don't know that Jo is short for a longer name. Thinks it long enough for *him*. *He* don't find no fault with it. Spell it? No. *He* can't spell it.

Dickens usually places direct speech in inverted commas; much of what the Coroner says is given this distinction. The more purely formal phrases, however, though evidently spoken, are not separated by inverted commas from the narrator's account, no doubt because they belong to the routine of the enquiry. It would seem, too, that after his summons to the boy, 'Now Boy!', the next sentences are unspoken thoughts, also in direct speech. When we come to the interrogation, 'Name' is spoken by the Coroner (though it might be the echo of this question in Jo's mind). From that point the questions are not given, no doubt since they belong to formal routine and can be inferred from the answers. All Jo's answers are given in free indirect speech. It is emphatically his language, his grammar, his pronunciation, but his words are given in the third person, and since he, in his actual answers, would stress 'me' and 'I', Dickens puts 'him' and 'he' in italics, thus evoking the boy's intonation. We can assume the verbs are also third person singular, though the common grammatical confusion between 'don't' and 'doesn't' disguises this.

The choice of this form for Jo's evidence, together with the neighbouring varieties of direct speech and narratorial report, arises out of the total context of the post-mortem. They reflect the jury's attention, single out what was significant for them. Perhaps it is the temporary adoption by the narrator of the jury's viewpoint that provokes so many cases of FIS in this chapter, in a book where otherwise it is not at all frequent. At the same time the FIS serves, as always, a double purpose. On the one hand it evokes the person, through his words, tone of voice, and gesture, with incomparable vivacity. On the other, it embeds the character's statement or thought in the narrative flow, and even more importantly in the narrator's interpretation, communicating also his way of seeing and feeling. The indirect form in which Jo's answers are given builds up a compassionate picture of the boy more strongly and surely than direct speech or any other form could do.

Though a few samples like these do not provide a sound basis for generalisations on Dickens's use of FIS, I believe that it does chiefly emerge in his work in situations like these—that is, when simple, rather inarticulate, uneloquent speakers are evoked, with a large measure of exuberant, grotesque, or compassionate mimicry. Very rare is its use for the more subtle reactions and thoughts of more complex, sensitive, and conscious minds; thus with Lady Dedlock FIS illuminates her inner anguish only faintly and transiently. The incidence and character of free indirect speech in the novels do, I believe, offer a clue to the frontiers of Dickens's imagination.

If we ask, why is there very little free indirect speech in *Bleak House*—and in Dickens's work as a whole—the answer cannot depend on any unawareness on his part of the potentialities of the device. We have seen how brilliantly he can handle it for certain purposes. We should, I believe, look for an explanation rather in the character of the stories he tells and more especially of the sort of narrative he invents. Its rarity in the first-person sections of *Bleak House* can readily be understood, even apart from the limitations imposed by the personalised narrator. For, even in the rendering of conversations, the use of FIS would impute too great a sophistication in the narrator, Esther, whose character is essentially modest, sincere, reserved, and unsophisticated. Making due allowances, this observation is valid for David Copperfield or Pip, too. But why is it relatively rare in the third-person narrative of *Bleak House?* I believe that it is the very exuberance of the narrator that prevents any lavish development of FIS here. I do not mean the obtrusion of the author himself, *in propria persona,* such as we meet in Thackeray or Trollope. I mean that exuberant imagination of Dickens in his role as narrator, as the impersonal medium of the story, that invents a world so rich in persons, situations, and incidents, all vibrating with potentialities. Any situation can, in his restlessly creative mind, develop infinite and potent radiations. Dickens, as a narrator, has so torrential a creativity that what any of his characters knows and sees and feels is slight and small compared with his vision. He cannot, like Henry James, submit to the guidance, the perspective of his characters and find among them voices to express his experience; if Dickens did so, the greatest part of his achievement would be lost. In *Bleak House* one only needs to consider the descriptions of the desolateness of London or Lincolnshire to be aware that no other form than the narratorial could have created these mental images.

This great quality of Dickens as a narrator is balanced by a limitation: none of his characters has the experiential and reflective depth, the moral awareness, of a Henry James character. Altogether, among his creations one does not find characters of great will and insight, absorbed in long-range purposes and of powerful intelligence, like Stendhal's Julien or Fabrice, nor characters of mighty, obstinate obsession, like Madame Bovary, characters capable of creating a mental image of the world that, however wrong, is comprehensive and coherent. Their absence reduces the relevance of free indirect speech, except for slight and incidental situations. It goes without saying that his complex and disorderly imagined world could not tolerate the use that Jane Austen, Goethe, and Trollope could make of it within a narrow, fixed, and definable social culture.

These seem to me to be the most important reasons for the relative absence of free indirect speech from Dickens's novels. There is a more technical one, too. With so complex and swift-moving an action or plot, which engages so many actors and fates, a firm narratorial line is a necessity. This is true also of Balzac and Stendhal. A Dickens novel arouses such a pressure of expectation, of dread, of hope, in respect to so many linked characters, that the delay involved in changing the narratorial perspective and dwelling on the subjective vision of a character is not over-welcome. The many-pronged thrust of the narrative will not tolerate obstruction for long.

The Thackeray-type narrator

There are many nineteenth-century novels in which the absence or relative absence of free indirect speech is significant. That it scarcely occurs in the novels of the Brontë sisters is partly due to the fact that most of these are first-person novels; but also, as Lisa Glaser remarks, its absence from *Wuthering Heights* corresponds to the mythical, epic quality of this work, which the psychological concern and complexity that FIS implies would undermine.[35] In some novels its absence might even be called a sheer loss. Thomas Hardy uses it very rarely, preferring the narratorial report, and there are situations in which the latter seems to cheat us of direct imaginative experience. When, in *Tess of the D'Urbervilles* (chapter 37), the sleep-walker Angel Clare carries Tess over the bridge, the narratorial account fails to evoke the intensity of experience that free indirect speech might.

The realism of Thackeray's stories, the social and psychological familiarity of his characters and situations, the leisurely pace of narration and confidential reflection, are all much more conducive to free indirect speech than the narrative modes of Scott, Dickens, or the Brontës. It does in fact occur fairly frequently in third-person novels like *Vanity Fair,* less frequently in first-person novels like *The History of Henry Esmond.* Always its ironic flavour is most marked and contributes to the general humorous–ironic relationship of the narrator to his characters. But, in *Vanity Fair,* the narrator has a double role. In one aspect he is the non-personal, ubiquitous, near-omniscient 'spirit of the story', the absolute authority. But in another he emerges as a much more personalised narrator, who may at any moment stand back from the story, address the reader as 'I' or 'we', confess to personal sympathies and antipathies, contribute explanations deriving from his personal knowledge, and add moralising comments that display the wisdom of a very tangible, rather worldly person. This narrator is so personalised that one might well call him 'the author'; we think of him as a man, not a woman, whereas generally neither 'he' nor 'she' seems to fit the non-personal narrator; he is tolerant, rather easy-going, decent, a man of the world who lives on a cultural and intellectual level above that of his characters.

Now, this more personalised narrator employs many of the typical indicators and forms of free indirect speech, certain forms of the verb, particles that refer to the perspective of the characters, and especially exclamations and exclamatory questions. These devices, however, have nothing to do with their function in free indirect speech. They are addressed directly from author to reader, usually as a means of enlivening the contact between the two, of prodding the reader's attention, inciting his involvement.

This double narrator is frequently to be found in the older novel, for instance in *Don Quixote, Tom Jones,* and *Tristram Shandy,* and the interplay between the two roles can lead, as in these novels, to a great enrichment of the art of story-telling. What we are faced with in Thackeray is, however, the use of free indirect speech in stories in which this double narrator functions, and in which we find that the frequent authorial interventions jostle with the FIS forms, sometimes to disconcert the reader, cheat his expectations, and confuse him.

77

I propose to examine these effects in two authors, George Eliot and Anthony Trollope, who in this respect clearly belong to the Thackeray tradition, but whose use of free indirect speech is on many occasions more subtle, varied, and essential than Thackeray's. Though their later work could have been affected by the practice of Flaubert, whose *Madame Bovary* (1857) was published at the time of their first novels, it shows little sign of any influence from Flaubert in any respect, including the use of free indirect speech.

1. George Eliot—author and narrator

In the novels of George Eliot, with their much greater concern for the moral quality of the characters than for external event, we might expect a profusion of free indirect speech, and it can indeed be found in abundance, from *Scenes of Clerical Life* (1858) to *Middlemarch* (1872), less frequently in the last novel, *Daniel Deronda*. It is almost always used to evoke the thought of characters, more rarely their actual speech. It can apply to any character and can fulfil many purposes, from simple humorous–satirical mimicry to the investigation of decisive moral choices. Situations of tension, of crisis, almost always rely on the reproduction through FIS of the character's view of the problem.

But the investigation of the moral issues, the tracing of changing attitudes and emerging decisions, are, like the structure of the story itself, very firmly conducted by the narrator, who emphatically establishes the moral values and judgements and the narrative perspective. This we might also assert of Jane Austen's work. But in George Eliot, as in Thackeray, this narrator has a double character, the absolute non-personal narrator on the one hand; on the other the author, very much like George Eliot herself, who uses 'I' or 'we' to address the reader, draws general conclusions, and establishes general truths (which could indeed be abstracted from the novels and published as *Wise, Witty and Tender Sayings from the Works of George Eliot*). Often the two roles merge. But at times, particularly in the earlier books, this 'author' takes on the features of an instructive social historian of provincial life, prepared to apologise for writing about uncultured characters (*The Mill on the Floss,* book IV, chapter 1); on many occasions she appeals directly to the reader—for instance, 'Do not think too hardly of Philip' (*ibid*, V, 3). This obtrusive author plays a very small role in Jane Austen's work, but in George Eliot's she never lets us or her characters quite out of her grasp. The great compensation for this unremitting intrusiveness is the quality of many of these comments, for they often delight the reader with their genuine seriousness, bright intelligence, imagination, wit, and pithiness that are their own reward. With this double narrator we are concerned here only in relation to the use of free indirect speech; we can confine our attention to *The Mill on the Floss* (1860) and *Middlemarch* (1872).

It need hardly be said that throughout, in order to evoke the inner life of the character, George Eliot uses extensive narratorial reports, descriptions, and comments, much dialogue, and inner monologues given the same grammatical form as direct speech, in inverted commas. Free indirect speech occurs frequently, in longer passages and short snatches, within the framework of the narratorial material. It is used for any character, though of course more frequently for the main characters, Maggie and Dorothea, since it necessarily implies a special concern for and intimacy with the character. The frequency of its incidence must affect the reader's response, since it tends to establish bonds not only of familiarity but also sympathy. It is significant that it is hardly used at all for Mr Casaubon, whom we get to know almost entirely through narratorial description and comment, through his occasional contributions to conversation, and through the medium of the other characters. The effect is a feeling that his inner life is secretive and alien, and perhaps hollow and unworthy of the reader's respect. Will Ladislaw, by contrast, is through the use of FIS recommended to our sympathetic attention from his first appearance, long before we have any grounds for believing he has an important part to play in the story.

The FIS in the novels is very varied. At its simplest it relies on mimicry of the idiom and voice of the characters, especially of the lesser characters, and consists of snatches woven into narratorial description. Though these characteristic phrases reproduce the thought or speech of these characters, we experience them above all as part of the description of manners. Typical is the passage on Aunt Glegg when she goes to view her sister's millinery (*MF*, I, 7, p. 53):[36]

> This was part of Bessy's weakness that stirred Mrs. Glegg's sisterly compassion: Bessy went far too well dressed, considering; and she was too proud to dress her child in the good clothing her sister Glegg gave her from the primeval strata of her wardrobe; it was a sin and a shame to buy anything to dress that child, if it wasn't a pair of shoes.

The characteristic phrases 'considering' and 'a sin and a shame', and the colloquial form 'wasn't' are the chief external signs of FIS here (we shall have to consider 'primeval strata' later). After the narratorial irony of the first sentence, the rest is FIS, with the appropriate past tense and third person; that Mrs Glegg thinks of herself as 'her sister Glegg' is an example of a fairly common literary device to avoid the confusions of 'she' in a context when both subject and object claim the same pronoun.

Such mimicry occurs frequently for the reflections of Mr Tulliver and of Tom as a boy, and for other secondary characters, as it does for Mr Brooke, Fred Vincy and other of the Middlemarch townsfolk, though it is much restrained in the later novel. The public reaction to Maggie's flight with Stephen is given in FIS form, with much mimicry of the clichés of the two opposing views (*MF*, VII, 2, 461–3). *Middlemarch* again shows less ebullience, and the common, conventional view of Dorothea and her marriage is expressed in its first chapter through the free indirect speech of one person, Mr Brooke, which embodies his peculiar speech-mannerisms. The mimicry itself can become quite complex, as in the case of the boy Tom, when comforting himself in the dreariness of school (*MF*, II, 1, 50):

> He was not going to be a snuffy schoolmaster—he; but a substantial man, like his father, who used to go hunting when he was younger, and rode a capital black horse—as pretty a bit of horseflesh as ever you saw; Tom had heard what her points were a hundred times.

Here Tom is adopting his father's familiar words, thus fortifying the compensating image of the 'substantial' man.

The degree of mimicry is a fair indication of the author's sympathies. It almost always has a humorous or satirical function, and in all cases where the full sympathy of the author is given to a character—Maggie when beyond childhood, Philip, Dorothea, Ladislaw, even Lydgate, or Gwendolen and Deronda from *Daniel Deronda*—there is no mimicry; the language of the free indirect speech used for their thought is close to the narratorial style, without peculiar idiom. Here we can more properly speak of irony, in the more profound sense that arises from the contrast between reality and the unavoidable and perhaps admirable self-delusions of persons imprisoned in the dimensions of individuality, time, and place. This the narrator makes explicit after a passage in FIS describing Dorothea's worship of Casaubon (*MM*, chapter 2, p. 44–5):[37]

> Dorothea coloured with pleasure, and looked up gratefully to the speaker [Casaubon]. Here was a man who could understand

the higher inward life, and with whom there could be some spiritual communion; nay, who could illuminate principle with the wider knowledge: a man whose learning almost amounted to a proof of whatever he believed!

The language is as much the narrator's as Dorothea's; all that is wrong about the thoughts is that the man admired is bogus. And, as if to stop us from smiling at the naivety of the last phrase, the author adds:

Dorothea's inferences may seem large; but really life could never have gone on at any period but for this liberal allowance of conclusion, which had facilitated marriage under the difficulties of civilisation.

Thus, if there is irony (and the exclamation mark after 'whatever he believed' is a rather broad authorial hint, while the preceding 'nay' belongs to Dorothea's thought), it is irony directed towards the inherent limitations and ruses of humanity.

At the opposite end of the scale from mimicry, FIS is used for the frequent evocations of inward struggle and spiritual search that attend most moments of tension in the novels. It is a prominent feature in Maggie's struggle with the 'temptation' of Stephen's wooing (*MF*, VI, 13, 432), of Dorothea's first realisation that Casaubon might wish to marry her (*MM*, 3, 50), of her first awareness of his hollowness (*MM*, 42, 463). The language of such passages sets problems that we shall return to later. It is less lively than Jane Austen's, much further away from actual speech and personal idiom; but it goes much deeper to the existential core of the characters, embodying the spiritual challenge that these heroines deliver to the common assumptions of their world.

Technically, the FIS passages are introduced most skilfully. FIS slips in and out of other forms, narratorial report or dialogue, without embarrassment; all that is needed is that the reader's attention should have been directed to the character from whom the FIS statements emanate. Often, like other writers, George Eliot makes use of exclamations and exclamatory questions to mark the transition to FIS, and the self-arguments of moments of tension and anguish are often conducted through a series of exclamatory questions—for instance, Dorothea's awakening to Casaubon's heartlessness (*MM*, 42, 463–4).

Often more subtle means are used to distinguish FIS, for instance verbal tenses belonging to indirect speech or verbs of inner argument and persuasion like 'might' and 'must'. Chapter 3 of book V of *The Mill on the Floss* opens:

I said that Maggie went home that evening [. . .] with a mental conflict already begun. You have seen clearly enough, in her interview with Philip, what that conflict was. Here suddenly was an opening in the rocky wall which shut in the narrow valley of humiliation, where all her prospect was the remote unfathomed sky; and some of the memory-haunting earthly delights were no longer out of her reach. She might have books, converse, affection—she might hear tidings of the world from which her mind had not yet lost its sense of exile; and it would be kindness to Philip too, who was pitiable—clearly not happy.

The chapter opens with the authorial 'I', the vocabulary and images are predominantly narratorial, and we are not sure whether the sentence beginning 'Here suddenly' is narratorial comment or Maggie's reflection. But 'might have', 'might hear', and 'would be' establish the passage as FIS, as her reflections rather than the narrator's, and the final 'clearly' has meaning only as Maggie's thought.

Similarly, after a narratorial passage describing Rosamund's schemes for getting her father, Alderman Vincy, to invite Lydgate to the house (*MM*, 11, 124):

She would not have chosen to mention her wish to her father; and he, for his part, was in no hurry on the subject. An alderman about to be mayor must by-and-by enlarge his dinner parties, but at present there were plenty of guests at his well-spread table.

This 'must' might indicate a general comment by the narrator, but the temporal adverb 'at present' combined with the past tense 'were' must mean indirect speech, a thought in the alderman's mind. As a consequence 'well-spread table', which if narratorial would simply convey information, gains in meaning, since it reflects the complacent self-congratulation of the alderman.

Generally, the use of tense shows a precise understanding of the functioning of free indirect speech. Celia's resentment over Dorothea's rejection of the devotion of Sir James Chettam, and her irritation over her sister's idealisation of Casaubon, are related in part narratorially, in part in FIS (*MM*, 2, 43–4):

Celia thought privately, 'Dorothea quite despises Sir James Chettam; I believe she would not accept him'. Celia felt this was a pity. She had never been deceived as to the object of the baronet's interest. Sometimes, indeed, she had reflected that

Dodo would perhaps not make a husband happy who had not her way of looking at things; and stifled in the depths of her heart was the feeling that her sister was too religious for family comfort. Notions and scruples were like spilt needles, making one afraid of treading, or sitting down, or even eating.

Until the last sentence, all this is narratorial report, interrupted by a scrap of direct speech. The past tense used for the generalisation of the last sentence shows it to be FIS, i.e. Celia's thought and images.

But there are occasions when a generalisation of this type, when in FIS, is more appropriately put into the present tense, as has already been discussed above (pp. 24 and 49). An example is found in *Middlemarch* in the paragraph following that just quoted. Sir James's attitude is being described, partly narratorially and partly in FIS:

As to the excessive religiousness alleged against Miss Brooke, he had a very indefinite notion of what it consisted in, and thought that it would die out with marriage. In short, he felt himself to be in love in the right place, and was ready to endure a great deal of predominance, which after all, a man could always put down when he liked. Sir James had no idea that he should ever like to put down the predominance of this handsome girl, in whose cleverness he delighted. Why not? A man's mind—what there is of it—has always the advantage of being masculine [. . .] and even his ignorance is of a sounder quality.

The past tense of the generalisation 'a man could always put down when he liked' clearly denotes Chettam's thought, i.e. free indirect speech. After the narratorial following sentence, the question 'Why not?' returns to FIS. But then the new generalisation about the advantages of the masculine mind, though in the present tense, is certainly no less subjective, i.e. FIS, than the preceding one. It would seem that, once the FIS mode has been established, the present tense can be safely used to convey subjective statements, if there is an advantage in so doing. For a generalisation like this, the present tense makes the assertion seem more confident and dogmatic, so that the narratorial irony behind it is more strongly felt.

The deictic adverbs 'today', 'tomorrow', 'yesterday', 'at present', 'ago', etc. are not, in George Eliot's work, sure indicators of free indirect speech. She uses them rather loosely, especially in the earlier novels, often replacing the subjective reference by an objective one ('that day', 'the next day', etc.). This lack of discrimination may be due to the liveliness of the author's imagination, which even in narratorial passages may fuse, through such an adverb, with the experience of the character. On many occasions, of course, the distinction is clearly made. Chapter 33 of book II of *Middlemarch* opens narratorially: 'That night after twelve o'clock Mary Garth relieved the watch', and when FIS takes its place it is introduced by 'She sat to-night revolving, as she was wont, the scenes of the day'.

With all this skill in the use of free indirect speech (awareness of which enriches, I believe, our understanding of the novels), there are two flaws, so persistent that they assert themselves as characteristic features of George Eliot's whole artistic conception and style. They stem from the same root, but can be discussed separately. The first lies in the language of FIS passages, the second in a stylistic confusion between objective narration and FIS.

In the first quotation on p. 79 above, the phrase 'primeval strata of her wardrobe' differs from the neighbouring statements. It does not at all bear the stamp of Aunt Glegg's mind and idiom, but is clearly the author's, who thus rather stridently makes fun of Mrs Glegg's parsimonious hoarding. The narrator's presence and irony are felt in the characteristic phrases of Mrs Glegg that are quoted, but with this phrase there enters a slightly jeering note, which is all the more disturbing because we are tuned by the context to expect some phrase of Mrs Glegg's.

This sort of disturbance of focus and tone occurs fairly often when the thought of lower-class and uneducated persons is given in FIS. We notice it after the quarrel between Tom and the poor lad Bob, who swallows his pride and picks up the pocket-knife he had angrily thrown back to Tom (*MF*, I, 6, 46):

> The knife would do no good on the ground there [...]. And there were two blades, and they had just been sharpened! What is life without a pocket-knife, to him who has once tasted a higher existence? No: to throw the handle after the hatchet is a comprehensible act of desperation, but to throw one's pocket-knife after an implacable friend is clearly in every sense a hyperbole [...]. Poor Bob! he was not sensitive on the point of honour—not a chivalrous character.

The opening tense of 'would', the exclamatory sentence, the rhetorical question, the exclamation 'No', all insist that the passage is free indirect speech. But the feeling and thoughts of poor Bob are mocked and jeered at through the smug elaborations of the narrator, which in form seem to claim to be Bob's thoughts. With 'Poor Bob!' the author emerges explicitly as a superior person.

Intrusive commentary by the narrator is of course frequent in George Eliot's novels, and its wit, profundity, and imaginative brilliance often fully justify its presence. As an accompaniment of free indirect speech it has a rightful place; but when it masquerades as free indirect speech and borrows its gestures, its legitimacy must be questioned. Even here, however, the questionable phrase may have such aptness or charm that it is more a gain than a loss. When Mr Brooke reflects upon his efforts to bring Dorothea to reconsider her marriage, his complacent thoughts, given in FIS, conclude (*MM*, 4, 65):

> In short, woman was a problem which, since Mr. Brooke's mind felt blank before it, could be hardly less complicated than the revolutions of an irregular solid.

The tense of 'woman was' indicates FIS, but the final image is obviously not Mr Brooke's; however, it is so delightful that no one could object to it, and in any case it does no harm to him in our minds.

This type of narratorial intervention creates a more serious problem in passages that present the moral struggle of the more complex characters. In their inner arguments, for which free indirect speech is largely employed, the degree and quality of the character's self-awareness is crucial; yet precisely this may be blurred by the form, the images, in which his or her thoughts are expressed. In the passage from *The Mill on the Floss* (I, chapter 3), quoted above (p. 82), the splendid image of 'the remote unfathomed sky' must be more an authorial reflection than a thought of Maggie's; if, as the style invites, we read it as Maggie's image, it gives a poetic elevation to her feeling of imprisonment that may be misleading. Or again, the reflections of Maggie before she is 'borne along by the tide' (*MF*, VI, 13, 432):

> There were moments when a cruel selfishness seemed to be getting possession of her: why should not Lucy—why should not Philip suffer? *She* had had to suffer through many years of her life; and who had renounced anything for her? And when something like that fullness of existence—love, wealth, ease, refinement, all that her nature craved—was brought within her reach, why was she to forgo it, that another might have it—another, who perhaps needed it less?

The series of exclamatory questions is typical FIS and used to admirable effect. One wonders, however, whether the enumeration of 'what her nature craved' is not more the narrator's rather sophisticated interpretation of her longings than her own reflection, and whether, if read as her consciousness, it does not suggest a more rational state of mind than the impassioned questions would. The passage continues:

> But amidst all this passionate tumult there were the old voices making themselves heard with rising power, till, from time to time, the tumult seemed quelled. *Was* that existence which tempted her the full existence she dreamed? Where, then, would be all the memories of early striving, all the deep pity for another's pain, which had been nurtured in her through years of affection and hardship, all the divine presentiment of something higher than mere personal enjoyment which had made the sacredness of life?

The passage continues with further exclamatory questions, one of which, an apex of her anguish, is put in the first person and inverted commas: 'Ah, God! preserve me from inflicting', etc. The series of questions indicates an inner monologue and is normal free indirect speech. But again we note, in the complex last sentence of the quotation, a contradiction between the tortured character and the language of her reflection, which suggests a plan of life and a capacity for judicious comprehension hardly reconcilable with Maggie's consciousness at this moment.

Such linguistic distortion, if one may call it that, is much less marked with characters like Dorothea Brooke or Daniel Deronda, largely because they enjoy a high degree of self-awareness and think and speak in terms very close to that of the narrator.

The second type of uncertainty of discrimination between the narratorial and the subjective perspective arises from the frequent use, for authorial comments, of the signals, the indices, of free indirect speech. Such intrusions cause no confusion when they are, as often, explicitly made in the first person as the comments of the authorial 'I' or 'we'; they do so when this is not the case, and especially when they occur in the neighbourhood of true FIS passages. The passage about Bob (*MF*, I, 6, 46), quoted above (p. 84), was there discussed as free indirect speech. But perhaps these exclamations and questions are not Bob's, but betray the lively engagement of a personalised narrator, as the phrase 'Poor Bob!' certainly does. All that one would then criticise in this case would be the use of the same stylistic forms for different purposes.

There are many examples of such authorial questions and exclamations whose sole function is to renew contact with the reader, kindle his attention, stir his sympathy, etc., and which lack any interpretative psychological function. When Stephen complies with Maggie's appeal for help (*MF*, VI, 12, 424):

> Stephen had the fibre of nobleness in him that vibrated to her appeal; but in the same moment—how could it be otherwise?—that pleading beauty gained a new power over him.

The question does not arise in Stephen's mind, as a self-excuse, but is authorial and, as such, superfluous if not misleading.

When Dorothea begins to realise Casaubon's hollowness, she goes to her boudoir, wrestling with tormenting thoughts (*MM*, 42, 463):

> She threw herself on a chair, not heeding that she was in the dazzling sun-rays; if there were discomfort in that, how could she tell that it was not part of her inward misery?

This question, despite the invitation to read it as FIS, must be authorial, since Dorothea is supposed to be unaware, in her misery, of the position of the chair. As such, it is purely rhetorical and tells us nothing about Dorothea.

Similarly, the adverbs that in FIS denote inward debate and uncertainty, like 'surely', 'perhaps', 'besides', etc., are also used in authorial comments. An excellent piece of FIS describes Maggie's remonstrance at her brother's harshness when he forbids her to continue meeting Philip. It is followed by a short paragraph that winds up her self-argument (*MF*, V, 5, 327):

> And yet, how was it that she was now and then conscious of a certain dim background of relief in the forced separation from Philip? Surely it was only because the sense of a deliverance from concealment was welcome at any cost.

The question, followed by 'surely', strongly suggests FIS; but the thought itself seems much more likely to be intended to be authorial. It is so important to know whether Maggie gained this profound insight or not that the uncertainty of ascription is a flaw.

Such uncertainties are not rare in George Eliot's novels, haunting some of the finest passage of free indirect speech. They are different from the sort of unavoidable uncertainty sometimes found in FIS which is due to the fact that it has no peculiar and unique grammatical form. The confusions discussed above are due to the continued existence in the modern novel—where subtle forms of free indirect speech are characteristic features of the narrative mode—of certain authorial forms that have become wellnigh superfluous, and that clash both with the FIS form and with the presupposition of a non-personal narrator.

The two 'flaws' that I have singled out both indicate a certain failure to discriminate between the perspectives of narrator and character. One of the stylistically most interesting passages in *The Mill on the Floss,* the description of Mr Tulliver's visit to the home of his impoverished sister and brother-in-law, reveals the same uncertainty (*MF*, I, 8, 70–1). The text is too long and intricate to examine here, and I must limit myself to a summary of the stylistic problem. On the one hand, one is struck by the brilliance that gives us, partly through the use of FIS, the picture of the landscape and of the negligence of the brother-in-law, as it takes shape in the mind of Tulliver, riding through the poor and barren countryside. But repeatedly the narrator takes over, and we are left uncertain, by the end, how much of the neglect, the dreariness, the poor husbandry of the farms, how much of the fecklessness and drunkenness of the local people, is registered by Tulliver. That George Eliot in some parts does build a picture of landscape and farm as it forms in Tulliver's consciousness is remarkable, and reminds us of the great achievement of her contemporary Flaubert. But this itself makes one regret all the more that the narratorial interventions, though adding information that is related to the theme of the visit, prevent the formation of a serene, visual and mental image that fuses landscape, character, and the character's immediate purpose.

What I have called flaws in George Eliot's handling of free indirect speech are slight compared with the great skill evident in its use—in its internal structure, in the interplay between it and other forms of narrative and description, its function at certain points of the narrative and indeed within the whole conception of the novels. The flaws are significant, however, for two reasons. At one level, they indicate a conflict between one type of novel—with its obtrusive author-narrator—and a more modern type, in which the story and the characters are much more entrusted with their own interpretation and message. At a deeper level, which may also have a historical significance but is certainly personal to George Eliot, the flaws arise from the unrelaxing determination of the author to insist on conveying certain moral judgements and conclusions, confidently to label certain types of persons and actions as good or bad, and to refuse the reader more than a modicum of freedom of judgement. Often one feels like begging George Eliot, 'Please leave the characters alone, to themselves, please leave us alone, to make our own conclusions.' This moralistic severity, which is of course evident in many ways in the novels, comes particularly into view in respect to the use of free indirect speech. It combats a substantial feature of FIS, namely, the more direct evocation of the character's viewpoint, which itself must imply a more generous appreciation of the variety of possible attitudes and responses in life. And though it does not mean the abdication of the author's authority, it does require a more gentle and subtle, a less dogmatic and self-confident, assertion of it.

2. Anthony Trollope—confusions of perspective

Free indirect speech appears in abundance in Trollope's novels, from the earliest to the last. It is already prominent in *Barchester Towers*, which was published in the same year—1857—as *Madame Bovary*; the later novel *Is He Popenjoy?* shows so lavish a use that one might almost believe the 'new' stylistic device was already in danger of hypertrophy. Trollope's novels do not make us think of Flaubert, either of the nervous and controlled artistry of his structure and style or of his implacable severity towards the world he evokes. Their tolerant, relaxed equanimity is also very different from George Eliot's strenuous moral engagement, and much more akin to Thackeray's attitude. His narratorial posture, in this like George Eliot's, also belongs to the Thackery type, and shows, though for different reasons, what difficulties arise when the intrusive author–narrator is saddled with the new responsibilities of free indirect speech.

The double narrator is often in evidence. Thus, in *Barchester Towers,* the author openly acknowledges his sympathy with Eleanor Bold (chapter 2) and his distaste for Mr Slope—'My readers will guess from what I have written that I myself do not like Mr Slope' (chapter 8, p. 55).[38] Fairly often the editorial 'we' is used in direct address to the readers. He may recall his own childhood experiences in Barchester cathedral (6, 43). But the narrator does not thereby become a fictional person with a defined perspective. Through most of the book he enjoys all the privileges of the non-personal, omniscient narrator, capable of divulging all secrets and enjoying an absolute authority in respect of the truth.

Trollope is by no means alone in mixing these two narratorial roles;

I have already mentioned (p. 68) that even such masters as Flaubert and Dostoyevsky do so. But the personalised narrator is much more obtrusive and active in Trollope's narratives than in theirs, and often, like Thackeray's, displays an assertive complacency that is very different from the humble role of the fellow-townsman of the Karamazovs. It is true that the novel is a very loose artistic form, and suffers far less from contradictions of style and clumsiness of composition than does the drama or the lyric. Perhaps this is due to its mere length, since, if the reader takes many days or weeks reading a novel, interrupted by many distractions, clearly its impact is so dispersed that a pure coherence of style is not decisively important. Its length may mean, too, that variety is as important as purity. One of the most intimate of forms, in the sense that reading is in modern times essentially a private act, it can profit from the renewal of contact between an author and his reader, even if this means that the mask of the narrator is lifted for a moment. It would therefore be pedantic and misplaced to criticise certain sorts of stylistic or compositional impurities, just because they are there. There are grounds for criticism only if the impurity means a confusion, and induces an error of interpretation. It is this type of confusion that occurs not infrequently in Trollope.

Corresponding to the contradictory types of narrator in *Barchester Towers*, a confusion sometimes arises between the narratorial mode and free indirect speech. This confusion occurs the more readily since the idiom of the characters, especially their vocabulary, is not conspicuously characteristic, and since the narrator's style is very close to that of his educated, somewhat genteel or would-be genteel fictional figures. In passages of direct speech or free indirect speech, expressive distinctions are given more through sentence structure than through vocabulary; usually the content is the most important clue to the identity of the speaker or thinker.

There are in this novel many skilled and effective passages of FIS, whether they are short touches woven into a narrative passage or a conversation, or longer stretches of reflection, akin to inner monologues. The account of Mr Slope's wily plans in regard to the bishop's wife shows several typical features of the style (chapter 4, p. 26):

> Mr. Slope, however, flattered himself that he could out-manoeuvre the lady. She must live much in London, while he would be always on the spot. She would necessarily remain ignorant of much, while he would know everything belonging to

the diocese. At first, doubtless, he must flatter and cajole, perhaps yield, in some things; but he did not doubt of ultimate triumph. If all other means failed, he could join the bishop against his wife, inspire courage into the unhappy man, lay an axe to the root of the woman's power, and emancipate the husband.

The verbs 'must', 'doubt', 'could', the adverb 'doubtless' all indicate the source of these calculations to be the character; the clerical and biblical tones make it still clearer, above all the swell of evangelical and moral conviction that justifies Slope's trickery to himself. Excellent too are such passages as Mr Harding's long rumination upon Slope's challenging sermon (13, 99–100), which presents in FIS the old man's distressed thoughts, alternating with incidental narratorial comments and refreshed by typical FIS indicators like the exclamatory question and ejaculations like 'Alas, alas!' or 'Yes'.

But there are many occasions when the style misleads. For instance, Mrs Bold's shock of surprise at Mr Slope's visit (8, 54) is admirably rendered in FIS introduced by a typical exclamatory question. But his success with her and her sister elicits the question, 'How had he done all this?', and this we find cannot be a question arising in Mrs Bold's mind, but is an authorial interposition, the purpose of which is merely to prod the reader. Or again, the questions signalling and accompanying Mr Harding's soliloquy (7, 48–9) lead to the exclamation 'Yes! all Barchester was in a tumult'; and this is, to our surprise, an authorial intervention. In the midst of a narratorial account of Slope's intrigues (24, 200–1), exclamatory sentences suitably denote the onset of FIS; but the author can use exactly the same form, as when he exclaims over Mr Quiverful's lack of spirit: 'Who can boast he would be better in such circumstances?' Equally troublesome is the use of the deictic adverbs of time. 'To-morrow he would have to declare . . .' (17, 134) is a true indicator of the bishop's temporal situation, and his ruminations continue in FIS, off and on, throughout his altercation with Mrs Proudie. But in the phrases that respectively open chapters 8 and 9—'Among the ladies who have hitherto acknowledged Mr Slope' and 'It is now three months since'—the time-indication is purely authorial, and 'hitherto' and 'now' only mean, 'so far as I have got with my tale'.

The association of different narrative perspectives may well enrich a novel, and in itself cannot be criticised. A reader can switch perspective without confusion. What is disturbing in Trollope's variations is that the use of similar forms for FIS and for authorial intrusions leads to real confusions, or to a disconcerting check to expectations raised by stylistic indicators. Trollope seems to be unaware at times of the psychological functions of the various forms, and one may discern a certain slackness of artistic attentiveness, an occasional sloppiness of craftsmanship, in spite of the often very skilful, delicate, and amusing writing. In large part the difficulties arise from the survival of the old-fashioned narrator, with his somewhat heavy-booted wooing of the readership (the French would call it 'bonhomie', the Germans 'Anbiederung'), that is misallied with the much more sophisticated narrative medium of FIS.

This personalised, obtrusive author makes far fewer appearances in the late novels, but a different sort of fault crops up. *Is He Popenjoy?* (1878) is a third-person novel of the normal type, in which a non-personal narrator enjoys freedom of access to the most private secrets of the characters and is the supreme authority. Throughout the work, the description of incidents is accompanied by accounts of what the characters are thinking and feeling, and all the main characters ruminate in a form approximating to the inner monologue, this being normally rendered in free indirect speech. Such a structure is logical and unexceptionable. Unfortunately this narrative pattern is so unrelentingly schematic that it becomes tedious, especially since much of the self-communing only reiterates what has already been made sufficiently clear through the behaviour, conversations, and earlier self-communings of the characters. Such overloading is possibly to be explained by the fact that the book was published in weekly instalments in *All The Year Round,* and Trollope either wanted to assure himself that readers had not forgotten earlier instalments, or found it convenient, when invention flagged, to pad out a thin instalment with self-communings. For instance, the reflections of Jack de Baron and of the Dean, at the beginning and end of chapter 54, are pure recapitulation.

However, these reflections are, throughout the book, of considerable formal interest, revealing a highly skilled use of free indirect speech and a characteristic confusion. They often embody the actual personal and class idiom, the psychological and social tone, of the different characters, catch delightfully a personal manner, even though they all belong to the same social stratum and share the same values. These FIS passages therefore greatly enrich the narratorial account around them. But also, we are often puzzled to know whether certain statements emanate from and illuminate a character or whether they belong to the observing author–narrator. Now, this uncertainty is a fairly frequent phenomenon in books where FIS is extensively used, and was commented on by Bally in his first articles. If Trollope is to be criticised on this score, the uncertainty of attribution must be of a specially disturbing kind. If, for instance, we sometimes cannot distinguish, in Thomas Mann's *Death in Venice,* the comments of the narrator from the views of the character, this is unavoidably so, since the grammatical form of FIS and of narratorial statement is basically the same, since narrator and character are so close to one another, in temperament and attitude, and since the narrator aligns himself from the beginning so closely with the one central character, Aschenbach. In *Is He Popenjoy?* the relationship of narrator and character is quite otherwise.

There are many characters in Trollope's novel, and though the narrator's sympathy is distributed in different proportions among them, he does not align himself with any particular person. Even with those who enjoy his greatest sympathy, Lord and Lady George, he remains morally at a distance, critical, even quizzical; appreciation is almost always associated with satire and irony, though the satire has the tolerance that might be expected in a narrator who, sometimes acquiring faint personal features, belongs to the same social class and culture as his characters. Perhaps the greatest weakness in the book is the easygoingness of the narrator, for he seems not to be deeply concerned over any particular fate, so that in the end we readers also do not passionately worry about what is to happen. But this indifference does not apply, of course, to the characters themselves, who in their reflections must and do take their own fates very seriously. If the narrator is in this way distinct from the characters, what he says needs to remain distinct from what they are believed to say or think; for that reason uncertainty of attribution of a statement is harmful. It is characteristic of this situation that Jack de Baron, the cynical, light clubman, and the time-serving, worldly Dean, are the characters best hit off.

The high quality and the faultiness in Trollope's style can best be examined through a rather lengthy extract from the ruminations of Lord George in chapter 32.[39] This virtuous but self-righteous man has been reproving his wife for her innocent friendship with Jack de Baron, but is himself enjoying a mild flirtation with Mrs Adelaide Houghton. Visiting his wicked brother, he is made indignant by a 'coarse and brutal' accusation against his wife's honour, determines to reject Adelaide's advances, and feels his heart 'softened' towards his wife. All this is told in a mixture of narratorial account and free indirect speech, and it is in passages of FIS that one most often strikes upon confusion:

> Why, oh why, had he allowed himself to be brought up to a place he hated as he had always hated London! Of course Jack de Baron made him unhappy, though he was at the present moment prepared to swear that his wife was as innocent as any woman in London.

The exclamatory 'Why, oh why' clearly indicates that the first sentence is free indirect speech. The following 'of course', a typical indicator of FIS, suggests that this second sentence too presents an inner argument of Lord George's, and 'at the present moment' seems to place us at his temporal standpoint. But this is a very odd phrase for Lord George to use, for what he is saying is that he is just at that moment ready to swear to his wife's innocence; the implication must be, he might not be able to stick to it at some later moment. Are we to believe, then, that Lord George is so sophisticated as to understand he may change, and yet to assert his belief? But throughout the novel he is very much of a simple-minded fellow, and his simplicity is in truth his redeeming feature. If we look more closely at this sentence, we are surprised to find Lord George thinking his wife as good as any London woman, for he detests London as a cesspool of vice. It is therefore clear that this second sentence is narratorial, not free indirect speech; it is the narrator who reminds us that Lord George was ready at that moment to believe in his wife's innocence, and that his trust was not likely to stand the test of time. But the narrator seems to have been infected by the neighbouring FIS and to have appropriated its indicators, 'of course' and 'at the present moment'.

The sentence that follows, which tells us of Lord George's decision to go to Berkeley Square, where Adelaide lives, and put an end to their flirtation, is clearly in FIS:

> But now, as he was so near, and as his decision must be declared in person, he might as well go to Berkeley Square.

'Now', 'must', 'might as well' all indicate that this is his thought; 'might as well' expresses particularly neatly the evasive way in which he justifies himself in keeping this embarrassing appointment. A few narratorial sentences then inform us how he discovers that by mistake he has put in his pocket a letter meant for his wife, and has given her an indiscreet letter of Adelaide's; she must by now have read it and would know of his 'affair'. There follows another passage, largely in

FIS, which again shows Trollope's rather slipshod handling of the style:

> There could be no doubt but that he had given Adelaide Houghton's letter into his wife's hands, and that she had read it. At the bottom of Hill Street he stopped suddenly and put his hand up to his head. What should he do now? He certainly could not pay his visit in Berkeley Square. He could not go and tell Mrs. Houghton that he loved her, and certainly would not have the strength to tell her that he did not love her while suffering such agony as this. Of course he must see his wife. Of course he must—if I may use the slang phrase—of course he must 'have it out with her', after some fashion, and the sooner the better. So he turned his steps homewards across Green Park. But, in going homewards, he did not walk very fast.

The first sentence is evidently Lord George's thought, FIS, while the second is narratorial. The question, 'What should he do now?' renews the free indirect speech; 'certainly' and 'could' indicate the argument going on in his mind, and the magnification of his predicament to 'agony' is neatly used to allow him to admit and excuse his lack of 'strength'. 'Of course he must' continues the FIS. 'Must' is in itself ambiguous, since it can mean either the (narratorial) 'was obliged to' or the subjective 'would be obliged to'; that it is here indubitably the latter is due to the effect of the preceding 'could' and 'would' and the neighbouring 'of course'. The last two sentences return to the narratorial mode. All this is excellent.

But we have ignored the parenthetic 'if I may use the slang phrase'. This phrase is extraordinary on several counts. This 'I' is not the non-personal, omniscient narrator, but a more personalised author, and as such scarcely appropriate in a passage where the most private mental movements of a character are being charted. But worse still, the author suddenly tells us, through this phrase, that it is he who is responsible for these words, this report, not Lord George, and in so doing he destroys the very illusion and function of free indirect speech, the more starkly since he uses a slang expression that would never be in the mouth or mind of the prim and prudish Lord George. The insertion not only destroys the perspective that belongs essentially to FIS; it also suggests that Trollope was not aware of the peculiar quality of this stylistic form.

A new paragraph then opens with an exact and delicate use of FIS, only to stumble once again:

What would she do now? How would she take it? Of course women daily forgive such offences; and he might probably, after the burst of the storm was over, succeed in making her believe that he did in truth love here and did not love the other woman. In his present mood he was able to assure himself most confidently that such was the truth. He could tell himself now that he never wished to see Adelaide Houghton again.

The two opening questions are emphatically free indirect speech, and so is 'he might probably'. In itself, 'Of course women daily forgive' could be narratorial, especially as the present tense is used, and if so would express the rather trite worldly wisdom of the sophisticated author. As a thought of Lord George's, however, it gains greatly, for it shows this prudish puritan, in his distress, clutching at the worldly wisdom he normally abominates; the use of the present tense does not clash with the subjective reference, but, as we have seen in other cases, gives a greater appearance of conviction to the thought. Since the following sentence begins 'In his present mood', we begin to read it as a continuance of Lord George's self-argument, for the deictic 'present' seems to indicate FIS. But we then notice that Lord George cannot both be 'confident that it was the truth' and conscious that it seemed so only 'in his present mood', since the latter phrase indicates that he may think differently at other times. This sentence therefore must be a narratorial statement, rather ponderously asserting the fragility of his conviction. One cannot help being misled by the form of the sentence, and hence being tempted to misread Lord George's character, and one must conclude that Trollope's writing is here rather slipshod and confusing. The confusion is typical, recurring frequently in this novel.

Trollope's stylistic skill and his faults belong together. The frequent use of the subjective statement, of free indirect speech, is characteristic of his tolerant concern for many different sorts of people and attitudes, his readiness to let them speak, to do justice to their inner arguments, whether verbalised or not. The narrator does not claim such moral pre-eminence as Dickens or George Eliot, nor do the urgent claims of his story, his plot—like Balzac's or Stendhal's or Dickens's—restrict the occasions when the characters may construct their own vision of their world. Trollope does not abdicate his rights as author; the narrator is always at hand, guiding the story and our evaluation of the characters, present also in the irony or sympathy that accompanies passages of free indirect speech. But he gives much space to the characters to express themselves, in conversations or letters and above all in FIS; and the last, since it adopts grammatical forms often indistinguishable from the narratorial, does sometimes give a higher status to a character's thought, attributing to it something of the authority of narratorial, objective statements. There is, in Trollope's imaginative conceptions, no subjective or sceptical uncertainty; the frequency of FIS demonstrates above all a generous, unassertive personality in the author, a wide appreciation of people (within the bounds of the class he describes), patience with variants from the 'good', with human frailty; a tolerance that is not unprincipled. But the slipshod confusions in his use of FIS? I believe these too stem from his tolerance and betray its weakness. For the ease with which he confuses narratorial and FIS statements, the contamination of the subjective statement by the personal author (and vice versa), is the fault of his tolerance. Especially in his weaker works, Trollope's imagination is not intensely absorbed in his creation, not profoundly concerned over the fates of his characters. He takes things too easily, acts the part of the clubman for whom too great a concern, too sharp a moral discrimination, is a burden to himself and others. Tolerance becomes mere live and let live. This is always a danger, in all his novels. It is significant that in his best novels, the Barchester series, or the political novels like *The Prime Minister* or *Phineas Finn,* where his sympathies are most deeply engaged, there is much less free indirect speech than in *Is He Popenjoy?*

VII

The French masters

Gustave Flaubert: *Madame Bovary*

First Bally, then Thibaudet and Marguerite Lips, and then countless other critics, including Stephen Ullmann, have examined Flaubert's style so skilfully, and found in it so abundant a display of free indirect speech, that it would be lost labour for me to try here to do justice to his brilliant handling of this device. However, no account of FIS can leave Flaubert out. It is not simply that he made discriminating, virtuose, and original use of its resources; with him FIS is explicitly bound up with his general artistic purpose. His avowed aim was to get away from the obtrusive narrator of the novel, the author who directs our attention, explains events and people to us, and proffers moral judgements. This was more than a revolt against the obtrusive personal author of the Thackeray type; it was also in a sense aimed at the impersonal narrator, the pure story-teller. Flaubert wanted to hide the very function of story-telling, as it were, to allow the story to tell and interpret itself, as far as this was possible; hence the narrator should, as he put it, 'transport himself into his characters'. Thus free indirect speech is not an occasional device, nor something employed for a specific situation or person; it is a major instrument for achieving the Flaubertian type of novel. Flaubert's realism did not imply the sort of objectivity that belongs to natural science, an objectivity founded on communicable skill and authoritative control over the (imaginary) object; on the contrary, it meant an imaginative self-submergence in the object, participation in the imagined character's experience, and communication of this intuitive experience.

This purpose and its realisation were so new at the time, so contrary to the normal expectation of a reader, that, where prominent indices were absent, it was often easy for contemporaries to take a subjective statement for an objective, i.e. to mistake free indirect speech for objective narrative. This mistake was made, perhaps innocently, by the Prosecution in the charge of immorality brought against Flaubert in 1857 on the publication of *Madame Bovary*, for Emma's rapturous thoughts as she sees herself in the mirror after her first adultery were quoted as being the direct observations of the author. Grammatically they might well have been so, but the Defence argued successfully that the passage only presented Emma's thoughts and gave no indication of the author's approval or disapproval. In its summing up, the Court, while clearing Flaubert of the charge, with some justice pointed out the dangers of a realism that abandoned the controlling observations of the author.

Actually, *Madame Bovary* does not abandon them, and Flaubert only imperfectly carries out his purpose. The author—narrator still remained, devising the story, imposing an over-all interpretation and meaning, more thinly disguised than Flaubert perhaps realised. And if FIS was one of the major devices by which narratorial report and explanation were supplanted, it was also one in which, as we shall see, the subjective perspective of the character is cunningly brought into the broader focus of the narrator's view.

I must content myself with a bare and schematic indication of Flaubert's use of free indirect speech, limiting myself to a few issues that are of the most general significance. The text of *Madame Bovary* will suffice for this purpose.

1. It has often been observed that in the first chapter of *Madame Bovary* Flaubert postulates a specific, personal narrator, a schoolfellow of Charles Bovary. This postulate immediately runs into trouble, for on page 5 the account of Charles's father and mother conveys personal information that no schoolfellow of their son could possibly know, and gives more, on page 8, in a passage of free indirect speech, including some direct speech of the father, that could certainly be known by no one other than the mother. It is therefore not surprising that Flaubert immediately dropped this fictive narrator, who disappears from the book with this chapter. The only reminder or legacy of the personalised narrator is the occasional reference to the 'present' state of the countryside as compared with what it was at the time of the story, the suggestion therefore that the story is being told by a real person about real events some time before. Even this is a little disconcerting, since the free access the narrator enjoys to the most secret recesses of personal lives is clearly a fictional device and can never apply to real life. Such references are more frequent early in the novel, for instance during the description of Yonville-L'Abbaye (Part II, chapter 2, 95–100).[40] The confusion, slight as it is, illustrates an important fact that has already been discussed. FIS is possible only in a very restricted area and sense if the narrator is personalised, whether he figures in the narrative as an active participant, or whether he is

only a reporter, a medium for telling a third-person tale. FIS belongs essentially to the third-person novel in which the narrator, depersonalised and impossible to name, has the right to enter into every mind and every closet.

2. In spite of Flaubert's intention to render the narrator invisible, there is much narratorial presence in the novel, both in the story-perspective and in moral judgements. Only a few examples need mentioning. The description of Yonville, already mentioned, is completely narratorial, presenting the place as it 'really' was, detached from the vision any character might have of it. An occasional sly comment, such as the comparison of the statue of the Virgin in the church with a Sandwich Islands 'idol', is an authorial piece of malice. Often the narratorial passages are loaded with valuation. The description of the committee of the Comices bristles with an irony that goes beyond what anyone present, I believe, would be tempted to (II, 8, 195 ff.). The first visit of Lheureux to Emma is accompanied by a narratorial sketch of his shady career and evil plans that reminds one of Balzac (II, 5, 143). Rodolphe's romantic costume is described with the fastidious distaste that clings to so much in the book, and transmits an authorial attitude, not the opinion of a character (II, 8, 191–2):

> His costume was an incoherent mixture of the everyday and the fastidious, in which the vulgar habitually believes it catches a revelatory glimpse of an eccentric existence, the disorder of passion, the tyranny of art [. . .]

> Sa toilette avait cette incohérence de choses communes et recherchées, où le vulgaire, d'habitude, croit entrevoir la révélation d'une existence excentrique, les désordres du sentiment, les tyrannies de l'art [. . .]

Towards the end of the novel the explicit moral comments increase in number, and there are such statements as 'she was corrupting him from beyond the grave' (III, 11, 472).

3. However, the characteristic feature of the novel, in spite of the fact that it does transmit the acrid taste of disgust, is the relative rarity of such narratorial intrusion. To a remarkable degree the characters are presented as they see themselves or one another; the landscape, the houses, are described in terms of their experience, their viewpoint. This can be done, of course, partly through narratorial description and analysis of their thoughts and feelings, partly through description of their behaviour, partly through their actual words in direct speech.

But FIS is also abundantly used to achieve this end, animating passages of description with the intonation and gesture of the character observing, so that character, setting, and event are fused. This can occur in small fragments that momentarily break into passages of narrative or dialogue; it can extend into longer passages, of inner monologue like Emma's dream of romantic happiness (II, 12, 271–2), or of description like the account of her visits to Rouen (III, 5, 363–5).

The brilliance of Flaubert's handling of FIS is perhaps most simply evident when there are no, or very slight, indicators of the onset of the style, when the reader is not shaken by an exclamatory phrase or ejaculation or a deictic particle out of the narratorial perspective into the subjective, but slips from one to the other, guided by only the most delicate hints. With Flaubert FIS is used fully consciously, asserts its natural rights, and needs no warning lights; it is a natural form of narration. The sophistication of the modern use announces itself. For instance, when Rodolphe rejects Emma's desperate plea to rescue her from her money troubles, telling her he has no cash available (III, 8, 429–30):

> He was not lying. If he had had it [the cash], he would have given it, without doubt, although in general it is unpleasant to perform such noble deeds: a request for money being, of all the squalls that fall upon love, the coldest and most devastating.

> Il ne mentait point. Il les eût eus qu'il les aurait donnés, sans doute, bien qu'il soit généralement désagréable de faire de si belles actions: une demande pécuniaire, de toutes les bourrasques qui tombent sur l'amour, étant la plus froide et la plus déracinante.

This is very close to narratorial style. 'Without doubt' suggests however that these thoughts may be running round in Rodolphe's head and are *his* sophistries; 'squalls' ('bourrasques'), a word characteristic of his man-of-the-world experience, confirms the remarks as his, as free indirect speech. What, if it were a narratorial comment, would be a somewhat heavy and platitudinous irony, is, as we recognise it to be Rodolphe's thought, a subtle evocation of his moral character. Similarly, the generalisation on the unpleasantness of doing noble deeds would be, if narratorial, rather trivial; as free indirect speech it is a characteristic piece of sophisticated cynicism from Rodolphe. If Flaubert had used the past tense for this generalisation, it would have been clearer that it is a thought of Rodolphe's, but the present (subjunctive) avoids some of the difficulty we observed in Walter Scott's use for a similar generalisation of the past tense. Like George Eliot and Trollope, Flaubert takes advantage of the freedom in the sequence of tenses that FIS enjoys (see above, pp. 49, 83 and 96).

Longer passages of a similar type are the description of Charles's first visit to Emma's father's farm (I, 2, 16–18), of Léon's visit to the church while waiting for his mistress to arrive (III, 2, 331–2), and of the journey to Rouen that Emma makes on her regular visits (III, 5, 363–5). These have scarcely any specific indicators of free indirect speech, and in form they are almost exactly like objective narratorial accounts, except in one respect. Flaubert is the first author systematically to use the past imperfect tense (the 'imparfait') for the free indirect form—of course not only for this purpose—and thus subtly to insinuate the difference from the narrative mode, which normally requires the preterite. Since Bally's first article on the 'style indirect libre', French critics have appreciatively analysed this stylistic resource, which is hardly available in other languages. Apart from this feature, it is essentially the content that establishes the fact that these passages reveal the objects and events concerned from the point of view of the responding character; perhaps the most decisive factor is the angle of observation. A smaller example demonstrates the method—the description of Emma as she walks with Rodolphe at the Agricultural Show, when he contemplates her out of the corner of his eye (II, 8, 188–9):

> Her profile was so calm that it could not be deciphered. It stood out clear in the light, in the oval of her bonnet, which was tied with pale ribbons like blades of reeds. Her eyes gazed straight ahead through her curving lashes and, although wide open, seemed a little hampered by the cheek-bones, because of the blood that gently pulsated beneath her delicate skin [. . .] Her head inclined towards one shoulder, and you could see between her lips the pearly tips of her white teeth.
>
> Is she playing a game with me? Rodolphe wondered.

> Son profile était si calme, que l'on n'y devinait rien. Il se détachait en pleine lumière, dans l'ovale de sa capote qui avait des rubans pâles ressemblant à des feuilles de roseau. Ses yeux aux longs cils courbes regardaient devant elle, et, quoique bien ouverts, ils semblaient un peu bridés par les pommettes, à cause du sang, qui battait doucement sous sa peau fine [. . .] Elle in-

clinait la tête sur l'épaule, et l'on voyait entre ses lèvres le bout nacré de ses dents blanches.

Se moque-t-elle de moi? songeait Rodolphe.

The wondering question of Rodolphe, so unemphatically linked to the description, makes it clear (if there was any uncertainty) that we have been absorbing *his* impression of Emma. The function of the passage is greatly enhanced when we understand its sensuous charm as his response, at this time intense and delicate, yet not excluding the rational thought of the calculating lover.

Such excellent interpretations of the quality of Flaubert's 'style indirect libre' are available, that I do not need to supplement them. However, within the general framework of a study of the theoretical problems arising from free indirect speech, Flaubert's practice gives rise to two that need to be examined.

4. The first difficulty arises from the interweaving of FIS and narratorial description. Once FIS has become of frequent incidence in a novel, once we have become used to descriptions that are projections from the viewpoint of a character, we tend to expect it everywhere, and may find it confusing if the objective, narratorial mode is used instead. This is especially likely when few and unobtrusive indicators accompany FIS passages. For instance, the description of Emma through Rodolphe's eyes that has just been quoted is shortly afterwards followed by an as it were balancing picture of Rodolphe—given above, p. 100. But the latter is narratorial, and embodies the narrator's fastidious distaste. The compositional parallelism of the two passages suggests we should attribute this harsh criticism to Emma, though of course it is utterly out of tune with her feelings about him. Similarly the passage where Emma, in the distress of boredom, looks out of the window at the clouds (II, 6, 167). This lyrical, poetic passage has little relation to Emma's thoughts and preoccupations at this moment, and seduces us to believe that she has the capacity to rise above her oppressions and sexual appetites and find an aesthetic solace in the colour pattern of sky and landscape. We have again to correct an error to which the style invites us. A comparable confusion arises in the description of Emma's visit with Léon to the wet nurse of her child, though the cause of the confusion is slightly different (II, 3, 127–8). This description can be taken as either narratorial or subjective; a 'turn to the left' which places the reader alongside the visitors is not decisive. The sordid details of the outskirts of the market town, the precision of the description of the wet

nurse's house as they approach—the patch of garden, the filthy drain-water, the washing spread on the grass, the neglected child—all register the revulsion of the elegant visitors and closely correspond to their experience. When they enter the single room of the cottage, the impression of neglect and desolation is intensified. But at this point the description becomes detailed, many items are mentioned—a page from an illustrated magazine fixed to the wall with sabot nails etc. Only after this description are we told that Emma picks up her child and begins to rock her in her arms. Here, an authorial interest in precise detail overshadows the experience of the characters, for we are surely not intended to believe that Emma is so heartless as first to scrutinise the contents of the room before rushing to pick up her baby, or at any rate that she would not immediately display her mother-love if only to impress her admirer. It would seem that here Flaubert's inclination towards realism in the more usual sense, a Balzacian concern for the social genre scene, momentarily thwarts his most characteristic artistic purpose, the construction of the mental world of his characters.

5. Such uncertainties occasionally involve a further problem that is inherent in the use of free indirect speech. It is a question of the language, the style, in which such passages are given. We have already seen what opportunities FIS offers for reproducing the gesture and in-tonation of a character, the vivacity of his peculiar personal expression, perhaps his slang, in contrast to narratorial description and simple indirect speech. This is especially the case when the actual speech of a character is reported in FIS, since the latter can utilise the elements that would also appear in direct speech, in dialogue for instance. It is not difficult, either, when articulate thoughts are given, since these also can incorporate characteristic turns of speech of the character. The distinctions are not so clear in older writers, like Goethe, where the speech of all characters is stylised and purified of personal, local, or class elements, and where the language of the narrator is close to that of the characters. Flaubert too does not allow his characters a highly personalised idiom, but usually, when giving in indirect style the words or articulate thoughts of his characters, provides enough of a characteristic tang to enable us easily to identify their source.

But this personalisation and differentiation is much less easily achieved when an author gives, through free indirect speech, the less formed, less articulated mental processes of a character, at a stage when they have not taken a recognisably verbal shape. It is an even greater problem when non-articulate reactions are to be given, when we are to experience the mode in which a character sees a scene, responds to a landscape, etc. When Emma looks out of the window, we might well ask, in what sort of words and sentences can what she sees be described? What does she see of the colours in the sky, would she think of naming them? Is she sufficiently aware of what she is looking at to register it in words? There is obviously no clear prescription in such cases, and the author has to invent a language of his own; on this particular occasion, as I have already suggested (following a critical comment by Marguerite Lips), Flaubert's language is misleading.

We can examine the famous, brilliant description of Emma's habitual journeys by coach to Rouen, to meet her lover and spend a day of luxury sealed off in the quiet hotel (III, 5, 365–5). She does the journey so regularly, the events repeat themselves each time so exactly, that one description does for all. As the coach sets off in the very early morning, the country is described from the point of view of someone accustomed to it, rather bored, impatient to arrive. There comes a pasture, then a post, then an elm, nothing to 'notice'. Emma always has a distinct awareness of the distance traversed, and even by closing her eyes cannot cheat herself into a pleasant surprise. Coming down the hill before Rouen, the city comes into sight, in a great bowl, and the extensive panorama is described, river, boats, factories, churches, smoke and mist. The precision and concreteness of the description corresponds to Emma's enlivened attention and anticipation, and as they enter the crowded city her excitement, growing, registers all the busy awakening life about her—clerks, shopkeepers, shoppers, cafés, whores—as she makes her way by devious back streets to the meeting place with Léon.

All the early and later part is flawless, illuminating both the journey and the woman making it. But the grand view of the city as the coach begins to descend the hill presents us with a problem:

> Dropping down in tiers and swathed in mist, the city broadened out beyond the bridges, confusedly. Further out, the open countryside rose in a monotonous movement till in the distance it met the blurred line of the pale sky. Seen thus from above, the whole landscape seemed motionless, like a painting; the vessels at anchor were piled up in one corner; the river wound round at the foot of the green hills, and the islands, oblong in shape, seemed to lie upon the water like great,

stationary, black fish. The factory chimneys belched out immense brown plumes which drifted away at the tip. You could hear the roar of the foundries together with the clear chimes of the churches that rose out of the mist. The trees on the boulevards, leafless, looked like violet bushes among the houses, and the roofs, all gleaming with rain, gave varied reflections according to their level on the slope. At times a gust of wind bore the clouds towards Saint Catherine hill, like aerial billows breaking in silence against a cliff.

Descendant tout en amphithéâtre et noyée dans le brouillard, la ville s'élargissait au delà des ponts, confusément. La pleine campagne remontait ensuite d'un mouvement monotone, jusqu'à toucher au loin la base indécise du ciel pâle. Ainsi vu d'en haut, le paysage tout entier avait l'air immobile comme une peinture; les navires à l'ancre se tassaient dans un coin; le fleuve arrondissait sa courbe au pied des collines vertes, et les îles, de forme oblongue, semblaient sur l'eau de grands poissons noirs arrêtés. Les cheminées des usines poussaient d'immenses panaches bruns qui s'envolaient par le bout. On entendait le ronflement des fonderies avec le carillon clair des églises qui se dressaient dans la brume. Les arbres des boulevards, sans feuilles, faisaient des broussailles violettes au milieu des maisons, et les toits, tout reluisants de pluie, miroitaient inégalement, selon la hauteur des quartiers. Parfois un coup de vent emportait les nuages vers la côte Sainte-Cathérine, comme des flots aériens qui se brisaient en silence contre une falaise.

It is a magnificent pen-picture, beautifully composed, each item a part of a visual pattern (with a sound accompaniment). The particular features—river, bridges, ships, factories, churches, trees, roofs, reflections—are distinct enough, but only distinct enough, to contribute to the whole composition. The rhythm has the composure, the completedness, appropriate to the contemplating artist, whose vision encompasses the whole, and it closes with a broad and entrancing image. One can imagine the observer standing to drink in the view, or recalling it in tranquillity. But Emma? rushing impatiently towards her lover? thinking of preparing her dress before leaving the coach, of excaping accidental meetings with acquaintances? When, in fact, she does leave the coach on entering the city, the description of her walk to the rendezvous is totally different in character, and genuinely interprets her haste, agitation, hopes. But in the splendid set-piece description Flaubert's aesthetic interest has overcome his artistic, he indulges his own response to the city landscape instead of constructing Emma's. The most striking evidence of this is the plethora of similes and metaphors. The chimney stacks emit 'plumes', the islands look like 'great, stationary, black fish', the clouds drive across the sky 'like aerial billows breaking against a cliff'. The differentiation of colours betrays a painter's eye, and 'varied reflections' from the roofs are explained in a way that would perhaps only interest a painter. All this is entirely appropriate as the product of an artist—observer. Not only is it questionable whether Emma Bovary would ever think in such terms, but a landscape painting like this surely misrepresents the state of mind in which she approaches her lover.

Such a criticism is valid only if the passage is to be understood as the response of a character, a participant, to the landscape. When virtuose descriptive passages comparable to this occur in Chateaubriand, or the Goncourts, or in Thomas Mann's *Death in Venice,* they are immune from such criticism. They are so too if, by one means or another, their quality as narratorial, objective, is clearly established, and differentiated from the subjective view of a character; as we have seen in several authors, an intertwining of objective and subjective statement, of narratorial account and free indirect speech, frequently occurs, richly profiting from the contrast and causing no confusion. I criticise the tendency in Flaubert because, since the prominent use of free indirect speech leads one to expect it on any occasion, and since there is a relative lack of signals of its onset, one therefore may be misled the more easily when a descriptive narratorial passage occurs. It would seem, indeed, that in the above passage, and on similar occasions, Flaubert's artistic intention is actually blurred, the authorial overlying the subjective, Emma's standpoint, which is the major impulse.

If the character-perspective of this passage be granted, is it properly to be reckoned to be free indirect speech? It is of course not reported words, nor reported thoughts, and could not be prefaced by 'she said', 'she thought', etc. Her impressions are recorded, the appearance of things as she sees them, and only through these, indirectly, are her emotive or nervous or mental responses conveyed. Perhaps it is stretching the concept of free indirect speech too far to apply it to such writing? I do not think so. For there is no definable line between this and the more declared forms of FIS, and when, as very often occurs in Flaubert's novels, there is no such stylistic flaw as in the passage criticised, it captures the essence of the free indirect form, namely, the reproduction of the inner processes of the character, expressed in the same syntactical form as objective narrative and embedded firmly in the narratorial account, but evoking the vivacity, the tone and gesture, of the character. It must be considered one of the signal achievements of Flaubert that he extended FIS to embrace, in this manner, those mental responses that are beyond (or beneath) verbal formulation and definition, that remain at the level of sentient and nervous apprehensions. In this he anticipates the major development of FIS in the twentieth century, for with Joyce and many other authors free indirect speech, though often present in the simpler 'classical' forms that we have already analysed, also often emancipates itself from the subordinate position of indirect speech and becomes identical grammatically with pure, objective, narratorial style. With them a process takes place that is the reverse of that criticised in the Flaubert passage, and we might say that the subjective view seems to usurp the authority of the narrator, for all we have explicitly presented to us is the experience of the characters, all that we directly know of their world is what emerges from *their* consciousness.

To return to *Madame Bovary*. The temporary supplanting of the character's perspective by the narratorial that has been noted in the last passage discussed occurs also in passages that are more indubitably FIS. When, as a young bride, Emma feels romantic longings (I, 7, 57):

Perhaps she might have wished to confide all these things to someone. But how find words for an intangible unease, as shifting as the clouds and whirling as the wind? She lacked the words, hence the opportunity, the courage.

However, if Charles had wanted it, if he had suspected it, if his eyes had chanced to meet her thought, it seemed to her that a sudden abundance would have dropped from her heart, as the ripe fruit falls from an espalier when one reaches out one's hand.

Peut-être aurait-elle souhaité faire à quelqu'un la confidence de toutes ces choses. Mais comment dire un insaisissable malaise, qui change d'aspect comme les nuées, qui tourbillonne comme le vent? Les mots lui manquaient, donc, l'occasion, la hardiesse.

Si Charles l'avait voulu, cependant, s'il s'en fût douté, si son regard fût venu à la rencontre de sa pensée, il lui semblait qu'une abondance subite se serait detachée de son coeur, comme tombe la récolte d'un espalier, quand on y porte la main.

It is perhaps possible to read the whole of this as narratorial; certainly the third sentence—'She lacked the words'—is narratorial. But the beginning 'perhaps' is idle if narratorial; if applied to Emma it is valuable as indicating her own uncertainty. The question 'How find words . . .?' ('Comment dire . . .'), if narratorial, is conventional rhetoric; but it fittingly expresses Emma's romantic feelings. The suppositions in regard to Charles might have expressed the narrator's opinion, but leading to 'it seemed to her' seem rather to suggest her own speculations; as such again they tell us not simply about his failings, but also her shifting of responsibility on to him. If these statements are in this way subjective, then so are the images; and to compare her malaise with the shifting clouds and the whirling wind is highly appropriate, for these are the images Emma would have picked up in the romantic poetry she preferred. But the lovely image of the ripe fruit, and the lyrical cadence of the phrase, seem to belong not to the oppressed creature but to the distanced author, and hence to bring a false note into the description.

My final example is pure free indirect speech, without any doubt. Emma has left Léon after one of their weekly meetings, and on her way to the coach sits down on a bench under the elms; she is in reflective mood (III, 6, 392):

    — Yet I do love him! she said to herself.

No matter! she was not happy, had never been happy. Whence did this insufficiency of life come from, this instantaneous decay of the things on which she relied? [. . .] But, if there were somewhere a being, strong and handsome, a valiant nature, filled both with exaltation and refined sophistication, the heart of a poet in the figure of an angel, a lyre with brazen cords, throbbing elegiac epithalamia up to the heavens, why then should she not chance to find him? Oh! What an impossibility! Anyhow, nothing was worth the trouble of searching; it was all lies!

    — Je l'aime pourtant! se disait-elle.

N'importe! elle n'était pas heureuse, ne l'avait jamais été. D'où venait donc cette insuffisance de la vie, cette pourriture instantanée des choses où elle s'appuyait? [. . .] Mais s'il y avait quelque part un être fort et beau, une nature valeureuse, pleine à la fois d'exaltation et de raffinements, un cœur de poète sous une forme d'ange, lyre aux cordes d'airain, sonnant vers le ciel des épithalames élégiaques, pourquoi, par hasard, ne le trouverait-

109

elle pas? Oh! quelle impossibilité! Rien, d'ailleurs, ne valait la peine d'une recherche; tout mentait!

This is typical FIS, following the direct speech governed by 'said to herself'. Emma's longing, impatience, vehemence, and disgust with her lot are present in tone as well as in content. The many exclamations and exclamatory questions obtrude her presence repeatedly. But the images? They express her dilemma with aptness and intensity, but they involve a power of generalisation, or distancing, that seems scarcely in Emma's power and her situation at this moment. In the last sentence, despairing and cynical, we hear her authentic voice; but the elaborate central sentence, with its highfalutin images and rhetoric, is not in keeping with her own mode of expression. Here again one must suspect that Flaubert substitutes his language and his perspective, and that means his mode of feeling, for hers. It is a sort of usurpation.

Narratorial usurpation is not the same as the narratorial presence that is often detectable in FIS passages. This, without distorting the subjective quality, inserts into it a narratorial tone, of irony perhaps, or humour, or sympathy. This narratorial tone can be produced solely stylistically, through the composition of FIS passages, the juxtaposition of its various items, or through its contextual relationships. In this Flaubert passage the composition admirably serves this purpose. The series of exclamatory sentences, the vehemence of the phrasing, the exaltation and the discouraged scepticism at the end, embody not only the tone and gesture, the attitude of Emma, but also in their condensed alignment, the pauseless juxtaposition of complaints and ideals, the narrator's implicit criticism of her romanticism and recklessness.

What I call usurpation seems to arise from Flaubert's obsession with style in the abstract, with 'le mot juste' and with structure and rhythm of sentence and paragraph, in the sense that, on occasions, when he is seeking to convey through FIS the character's own perspective, his feeling of 'rightness' is determined not so much by the specific situation of the character as by the contemplating narrator, or perhaps here we should say, by the author. For Hugo Friedrich understands this unremitting search for 'le mot juste', this obsessive artistry, as Flaubert's means to counterbalance the world for which he felt such bitter distaste, to 'exorcise' the hateful, inane world he evokes in his novels.[41] In the purely narratorial sections of the novels, such an intention can scarcely be criticised from a formal point of view. But where it asserts itself in passages which purport to reproduce the attitude and vision of characters, it is not only confusion but a threat to a very delicate nerve of the work, since it may impute to a character—Emma Bovary, for instance—an aesthetic compensation she is far from seeking or feeling.

I make so much of this fault in an author whose handling of FIS is in general so brilliant because it arises from a problem that has often made itself felt since his time, in the writing of novelists concerned to suppress as far as possible the narrator's voice and role and to speak through their characters' consciousness. The purpose itself, if carried through to its extreme, imposes a great limitation on what may be written, since only that is legitimised that registers through the sensibility of the characters. Henry James often spoke of this problem, concluding that, because of this, it was necessary for the author to create a central character (or characters) sensitive and intelligent enough to interpret adequately the whole range of implication of the imagined situations and story. But this solution meant that only a certain type of person may be placed at the heart of a narrative. What should be done if the imagined story was to be built round persons without this awareness, sensitivity, and moral concern? We can trace how Joyce solved this problem in *Ulysses*; but occasionally, for instance in *A Portrait of the Artist*, he shows a certain dissatisfaction with the limits his method sets, and indulges in 'fine' writing that is hardly appropriate. Faulkner also, if in three sections of *The Sound and the Fury* he speaks through fictional characters, only in the fourth, narratorial section can allow himself a more complex, subtle style that discovers words for much that up to then was mute and inarticulate. In many modern novels we never escape from the confines of the restricted mentality of the characters. The nineteenth-century novel, however fully it might adopt the character-perspective implied by FIS, never abandoned an accompanying and controlling narrator-perspective, and therefore did not suffer from the modern limitation.

In spite of the limitations that may arise from the extended use of free indirect speech, it is also clear, from a study of Flaubert's work and the other novels so far discussed, what extraordinary freedoms inhere in this form of indirect speech. By the term 'free indirect style' Bally meant to indicate certain freedoms that in English or German do not seem so distinctive; it is for other reasons that the term seems highly appropriate. FIS allows an extraordinary freedom in tense and sequence of tense; it allows for great freedom in the arrangement and composition of different items of an extended reported statement or thought; it can so far free itself from the status of 'indirect' that it can often closely approximate in form to the objective narratorial statement, and can seem to acquire the authoritative status of the narrator's own account. Its idiom, though in one way or another evoking the character, also offers great choice, since on many occasions, and especially for the presentation of non-articulate thoughts and impressions, the narrator must provide a language for matters that, for the character, resist verbal formulation and, with that, characteristic expression. When we compare free indirect speech with direct speech or simple indirect speech, these great freedoms stand out and proclaim its extraordinary versatility.

Emile Zola—use and abuse

When Zola is mentioned by Bally or Lips it is usually with the intention of criticising him for having vulgarised the use of free indirect speech, for having turned it into a mannerism. It is true that Zola does use it very freely, and sometimes rather indiscriminately, but he also uses it very skilfully and effectively. It is worth examining both the good and the bad aspects since his usage seems to have had a particular influence on the European novel, and also throws some light on his theoretical conception of realism. Marguerite Lips herself, though she calls the 'style indirect libre' an 'obsession' with Zola, quotes with approval a magnificent passage from *L'Assommoir*. To some extent her and Bally's criticism may have been due to their distaste for the sordid aspects of Zola's realism; passages can often be identified as FIS because the crude obscenities betray their source as a character's words or thought. In addition Bally (as noted above, p. 17) draws attention to Zola's exploitation of FIS as a means to smuggle in his own viewpoint under the mask of a character. His irritation at Zola's habit, in *Rome*, of always describing the city through the medium of a character's consciousness is less well founded.[42]

The claim that Zola made in his theoretical essays, that the novelist is the equivalent of the natural scientist, explains in part the status and role of the narrator in his novels. He is not obliterated, since he is guiding an 'experiment'. That is, the author defines the experiment, invents the characters in their social setting, establishes their relationships, and through the medium of the narrator constructs a story that will lead to a conclusion that demonstrates some general truth about social and personal psychology. The author is in one sense not objective, since he is deeply concerned over the moral and social issues. But his engagement is not expressed through personal sympathies, sentimental preferences, or moral bias—at least, this is Zola's intention. His realism resides in his objectivity, or rather the objectivity of his narrator, the truth of his investigation. Zola was sometimes aware that such 'investigations' are inevitably more subjective than those of the natural scientist, hence his famous qualification that art presents 'a corner of nature seen through a temperament'. But in general he seems to have considered the artist's temperament to be a regrettable necessity, and to have approximated as closely as he could to the position of the scientist. The normal structure of his novels illustrates this attitude. The narrator, an impersonal intelligence, distinct and remote from his characters, is in possession of the authoritative truth about them and their environment. Descriptions and reports of persons, scenes, and events are in the main narratorial, telling us what they 'really' are, as distinct from what the characters may think or say about themselves and the world about them. The narrator may also add psychological, sociological, or ethical comments to explain the course of events and draw conclusions.

But Zola's theory of the artist–scientist does not prepare us for another prominent feature of his writing, the free indirect speech that abounds in it. For Zola does not only present the human world as a natural scientist might, but he gives us too the images that the characters form of life. His narrator depends only partly on observation, for he also works through intuition, through imagination and sympathy; if his creation is to be full and true, he has to make use of the power to imagine the secret vision and thought within a character, the images that haunt the mind, as well to take in the behaviour that makes impact on an external observer. This power of intuition, always postulated by free indirect speech, is often evident in Zola's works. If it makes the analogy with the natural scientist highly questionable, it does not in itself conflict with the concept of objective truth, though it makes this truth far more complex, since it is made up both of the authoritative truth available to the narrator and the partial truths and limited reality that each person carries round with him. It is true that Zola reconciles these two truths, the objective and subjective, since the narrator's truth comprehends and transcends the partial truths of the characters. But at times the narrator's view seems to withdraw in face of the perspective of a character—notably, for instance, in the closing pages of *Germinal*—and we seem to glimpse a problem that Zola himself was not theoretically aware of, but that imposed its urgency in the twentieth century. This arises from scepticism concerning the whole postulate of an omniscient, authoritative narrator, a postulate for which there is no parallel in reality, and the consequent search for a form of narrative that confines itself to the more human, natural dimensions of experience as it may be known to a real person.

These considerations lend a wider interest to the examination of Zola's use—and abuse—of FIS. We need only concern ourselves with a few typical examples, and I propose to restrict my observations to *Germinal* (1885) and *Earth* (*La Terre*, 1887).

In these novels FIS occurs so frequently that the reader has to be on his guard not to mistake straightforward narratorial statements for subjective. Sometimes, indeed, narratorial statements bear the typical indicators we associate with FIS, this being the result not of infection by FIS but of the survival of the older personalised narrator that we have noted in Thackeray. In the free indirect speech there is generally an abundance of the indicators that Bally and Lips identified: the exclamation or exclamatory question frequently introduces FIS, often in the form of brief ejaculations like 'yes!' or 'no matter!' ('oui', 'n'importe'); particles of inward argument like 'so', 'doubtless', 'besides' ('donc', 'sans doute', 'd'ailleurs') are freely scattered about; and verbs of obligation and persuasion like 'might', 'must', 'ought' ('pouvait', 'devait') are used with a subjective reference. In addition, and much more frequently than in earlier authors, the vocabulary often indicates unmistakeably the person thinking or speaking. Since the characters in these novels are for the most part miners or peasants, these passages (of direct speech as well as of free indirect speech) stand out through their crudity, vehemence, and often obscenity.

Hence the vehemence of Catherine's fury and despair (*Germinal*, VI, 5, 484–5).[43]

> She [Catherine] was choking, she was bursting with the craving to slaughter everybody. Wouldn't it all soon be over, this accursed life of misery? She had had enough of being beaten and chased off by her man, of floundering about like this.

> Elle suffoquait, elle crevait d'une envie de massacrer le monde. Est-ce que ça n'allait pas être bientôt fini, cette sacrée existence de malheur? Elle en avait assez, d'être giflée et chassée par son homme, de patauger ainsi.

The exclamatory question of the second sentence shows the passage to be FIS; we then perceive that the words 'choking', 'bursting', 'slaughter', etc. belong to Catherine and express *her* fury, while the structure of the last sentence, its disjointedness, express *her* mode of awareness of her desperation. The narrator is here not giving her actual speech; his role is to condense the turmoil of resentments whirling in Catherine's head and order them in the most convincing form.

Another typical example of FIS, when an external occurrence, narratorially told, sets Etienne off on a customary political oration (III, 3, 186):

> That would set Etienne going. What! wasn't the worker allowed to think for himself! Eh! that's why things would soon be changing [. . .]

> Du coup, Étienne s'animait. Comment! la réflexion serait défendue à l'ouvrier! Eh! justement, les choses changeraient bientôt [. . .]

These excited exclamations introduce a long passage of FIS, providing the hinge on which we swivel from the narratorial to the subjective mode.

The signals of FIS are not always so blatant. Often it is the content, or the vocabulary or unemphatic particles, that assure us that a passage is subjective, not narratorial. When Catherine is trying to stop her young brother and his girl accomplice from looting (III, 2, 172):

> All Catherine could do was box her brother's ears, the little girl was already galloping away with a bottle. These diabolical kids would end up doing hard labour.

> Catherine ne put que gifler son frère, la petite galopait déjà avec une bouteille. Ces satanés enfants finiraient au bagne.

When the miners are celebrating at the fair (III, 2, 174):

> It was now Maheu's turn to stand drinks. After all, if the lad wanted to avenge his sister, it wasn't a bad example to give. But Philomène's mind was at rest now, since she had seen Moquet, and she wagged her head. Those two buggers had sure enough gone to the Volcano.

> Maheu, à son tour, offrait des chopes. Après tout, si le garçon voulait venger sa sœur, ce n'était pas d'un mauvais exemple. Mais, depuis qu'elle avait vu Moquet, Philomène, tranquillisée, hochait la tête. Bien sûr que les deux bougres avaient filé au Volcan.

Narratorial style and FIS are closely intertwined in both passages. In the second example the first and third sentences are narratorial, while the second gives Maheu's thought and the fourth Philomène's. The words indicating an inner argument are, apart from the obscenity 'bougres', the only indicators of FIS ('after all' and 'sure enough').

Earth and Zola's other novels show an abundance of such passages, all adding great vivacity to the description since they present the story, repeatedly, in terms of the characters' awareness. At the same time, the FIS does not simply evoke the peculiar identity of the character. As compared with direct speech, or simple indirect speech, it allows for selection by the narrator, condensation, composition, for what we are given is the gist of what is thought or said, not the full rambling inconsequence of reflection. In this respect, therefore, FIS does not solely facilitate in the reader the direct 'experience' ('Erleben') of the character's situation, for it is also a means whereby the author draws the character into the narrator's focus, sharpens his profile, illuminates an aspect. The fact that pieces of FIS are intertwined with the objective narrative also means that the subjective responses are ordered within the narrator's overriding perspective. In general Zola's use of FIS in *Germinal* is very skilful, both in respect to its inner structure and to its contextual integration. One might object to it only that it is somewhat too blatantly signalled, that it occurs almost too frequently, and that the author seems to enjoy taking advantage of it to introduce rather drastic obscenities.

We need here examine only one other example, to which there are parallels in several other Zola novels. The ending of *Germinal* describes the central character leaving the scene of events, and reflecting on what he has experienced. In all such situations in Zola's novels, FIS is used rather more lavishly than elsewhere, to give as it were a final tableau. These last pages of *Germinal* are justly famous, particularly for the prophecy of the inevitable workers' revolution that will put an end to exploitation, which has often been understood as a personal profession of faith by the author. In fact, what we are presented with here is the faith of Etienne, and since we have earlier been informed that he bears the pathological legacy of the Rougon-Macquarts in his temperament, we might view his faith with some scepticism. The misreading of these last paragraphs is largely due to a failure to recognise the form of free indirect speech.

At times the description of Etienne's journey to the railway station is narratorial. At most there is a certain alignment of the focus beside him, with such comments as 'on the left' ('Etienne turned to the left

116

along the road to Joiselle'). As he walks, the description of the industrial mining landscape amidst the smiling spring countryside is given from his point of view, but is narratorial in form. Then comes free indirect speech, introduced with typical exclamations (VII, 6, 588–91):

> Yes, Mother Maheude with her good common sense put it well, that would be the great victory [. . .] Ah! what an awakening of truth and justice! The crouching, sated god would instantly perish, that monstrous idol hidden in the depths of his tabernacle, in that remote mystery where he is fed on the flesh of the poor, who have never seen him.

> Oui, la Maheude le disait bien avec son bon sens, ce serait le grand coup [. . .] Ah! quel réveil de vérité et de justice! Le dieu repu et accroupi en crèverait sur l'heure, l'idole monstrueuse, cachée au fond de son tabernacle, dans cet inconnu lointain où les misérables la nourrissaient de leur chair, sans l'avoir jamais vue.

The thoughts, the utopianism, the simplifications, the rhetorical clichés and tone, are all the stock-in-trade of the political agitator and clearly belong to Etienne.

His journey proceeds, told narratorially, with more directional indications—'to the right', 'opposite'—to keep the reader close beside him. His need to hurry is more urgently felt by us because it is given in FIS:

> If he wanted to catch the 8 o'clock train he had to hurry, for he still had six kilometres to walk.

> S'il voulait ne pas manquer le train de huit heures, il devait se hâter, car il avait encore six kilomètres à faire.

Here we recognise FIS because of 'wanted' and 'had to', in the imperfect tense in the original.

And this leads to the famous final paragraph, in which Etienne hears in his imagination, 'beneath his feet', the picks of his comrades down in the mines, and the swelling noise seems to break through the crust of the earth as the spring grain and buds burst the husks of winter, foretelling the coming of

> a black, avenging army that was slowly germinating in the furrows, swelling for the harvests of the coming century, whose germination would soon crack the earth asunder.

une armée noire, vengeresse, qui germait lentement dans les sillons, grandissant pour les récoltes du siècle futur, et dont la germination allait faire bientôt éclater la terre.

There can be no doubt that these final passages, containing both narratorial and FIS forms, convey Etienne's thoughts and longings; all the stylistic marks are present.

In his first criticism of Bally's definition of free indirect speech, Kalepky posed another interpretation. He recognised that FIS is used by Zola, but asserted that he merely made the character his mouthpiece. Is this so here? The passage does show a broad humane sympathy in the narrator for the sufferings and aspirations of the miners for liberation, sympathy for Etienne's feeling of solidarity, too. We can also hear irony in the stereotyped clichés of Etienne's dream of revolution. But there are no intrusive opinions of the narrator, no sleight of hand that might slip in an authorial opinion or even confirmatory guarantee under cover of the character. The attitude expressed in these last pages is homogeneous and fully fits Etienne's personality. The question as to whether this prophetic vision of his is shared by the author cannot be decided from these last pages alone, but only from the totality of the book, from the experiences undergone and the conclusions reached by the character, from the reliability of the character of Etienne as have learned to know it. We should then be judging the author on the evidence of the totality of his vision, or rather, we should be assessing the quality of this vision, not something else, his opinions, detached from the work itself.

The skilful use of FIS in *Germinal,* as in the earlier *L'Assommoir* (1877), scarcely deserves the rather sharp criticism of Zola that we find in Bally or Lips. But *Earth (La Terre),* though published in book form only two years after *Germinal,* offers stylistic evidence of a considerable deterioration in Zola's artistry that is particularly striking in his handling of free indirect speech (there is a similar deterioration in composition, too). The flaws may be summed up under three main heads:

1. The descriptions of the rural landscape are almost all authorial. They are often sophisticated word-pictures, compositions of colour and masses, that convey a mood, usually the mood of an outsider to the story, an artist—observer. These descriptions present the setting for the characters, predominantly peasants, and often the two are incongruous, for the landscape so sophisticatedly described is not that that the peasant observes and experiences. For instance, when Jean

brings the peasant Mouche, who has had a stroke, to the latter's farm, and looks round this unfamiliar place to see where he should take the sick man, the expressive description of the neglected farmstead misleads the reader about Jean's reactions.[44] Zola seems often unable to resist the lure of fine writing, and though this may not necessarily and always be inappropriate, it may infect the passages in FIS themselves. When M. Charles, the bourgeois rentier, a pillar of respectability and former brothel-owner, describes Chartres (where his business was), his description is properly endowed with pretensions to aesthetic, moral, and religious refinement, especially as he is showing off before an attractive woman. But how could such a man, in a passage of free indirect speech introduced by 'Yes, one of the most beautiful monuments', use, when speaking of the cathedral square, expressions like these (p. 188):

the deserted square, crossed on weekdays only by the shadows of the faithful; and, that sadness of great ruins, he had felt it, one Sunday when, passing by, he had gone in just at the time of vespers [. . .] small girls, lost there like a handful of ants, it wrung your heart [. . .]

la place déserte, que seules les ombres de dévotes traversaient en semaine; et, cette tristesse de grande ruine, il l'avait sentie, un dimanche qu'il y était entré, en passant, au moment des vêpres [. . .] petites filles, perdues là comme une poignée de fourmis, ça serrait le cœur [. . .]

The combination of evocative skill and rather heavy irony is such as to allow one to understand why Kalepky could consider free indirect speech to be a trick to smuggle in authorial opinion.

2. The narrator in this novel, as usually with Zola, is non-personal. But the narratorial passages sometimes express this impersonal narrator's emotional engagement in events, sometimes directly through affective exclamations. The sort of confusion that results from this double role of the narrator has already been discussed in reference to George Eliot and Anthony Trollope. In *Earth* we read, after the description of the rich farmer Houdequin's worries (pp. 99–100): 'Ah, this land, how he had come to love it!' We take this as a normal introduction of a FIS passage, the exclamatory 'Ah' helping us to see in the phrase Houdequin's self-communing. But it continues: 'and with a passion which was more than the acrid avarice of the peasant, with a sentimental passion': 'Ah, cette terre, comme il avait fini par l'aimer! et

d'une passion où il n'entrait pas que l'âpre avarice du paysan, d'une passion sentimentale'. The last sentence clearly is the judgement of an onlooker, and we must presume that the first 'Ah' is also an expression of the narrator's feeling. Lower down on the same page we read: 'No matter, he would remain the prisoner of his land', which is true FIS. Such sympathetic expressions of the narrator, accompanied by indicators typical of FIS, are confusing in the sense that they subliminally exert illegitimate and distorting pressure on the reader's response.

3. Such emotional participation by the author–narrator may indicate a certain insecurity in the whole artistic stance of the narrator. In *Earth* it betrays the fact that the author is less deeply identified with events than in *Germinal,* less at home with his characters, and feels himself more of an outsider, an investigator and reporter. At the same time, he is equally interested to admit us, through free indirect speech as through other devices, to the intimacy of the characters' feeling. But, even in passages which do convey their experience, flaws may arise. When the immediate result of the old peasant Fouan's distribution of his land among his children is described, FIS is admirably used to show how Fouan and his wife Rose cover over their dismay by praising the advantages of being retired and idle (p. 132). Rose begins, in indirect speech:

> 'Truly! they had really earned it [. . .] Getting up late, twiddling their thumbs [. . .] Ah! it was a thorough change, they were in paradise, for sure.'

> 'Vrai! ils avaient bien gagné ça [. . .] Se lever tard, tourner ses pouces [. . .] ah! ça les changeait rudement, ils étaient dans le paradis, pour sûr.'

The narrator describes how Fouan joins in:

> He himself, livened up, got excited like her, outbid her [. . .]

> Lui-même, réveillé, s'excitait comme elle, renchérissait [. . .]

But then comes:

> And underneath this forced rejoicing, underneath the fever of what they were saying, one could feel deep trouble [. . .]

> Et, sous cette joie forcée, sous la fièvre de ce qu'ils disaient, on sentait l'ennui profond [. . .]

Who is this 'one'? It is certainly not the family or the neighbours, all convinced of the desirability of a rentier existence, and in any case not present here. It is the narrator, speaking for himself and on behalf of the readers, and yet in a form which suggests his presence and participation in the fictional events. This tendency often develops into a sort of 'bonhomie' of understanding between narrator and reader, so that the 'doubtless' or 'besides' characteristic of FIS sometimes only function as an aside from narrator to reader.

The ending of *Earth,* apparently echoing the magnificent close of *Germinal,* shows the same confusion, and here one can accuse Zola of using a character as a powerful instrument to drive home his own, authorial interpretation of the story. It is comparable to the endings of the late novels *Rome* and *Lourdes* that Bally criticised; and though the following passage is not actually in FIS form, an analysis shows an abuse that often occurs in FIS passages.

Jean Macquard, a former soldier who has been trying to settle in the village, is leaving the scene of implacable greed and brutal conflict to enlist again; a simple, honest fellow, he is appalled at the crimes, viciousness, and suffering he has witnessed. As he departs, we are given his 'maundering reverie' ('rêvasserie confuse', pp. 517–19). His thoughts circle round the brutality that the greed for land engenders, and turn to the contrast between these 'quarrels of raging insects' and the constancy of the fertile earth. He reflects:

> What does our misfortune weigh in the great mechanism of stars and sun? He makes fun of us, that dear God of ours! We win our bread only by a terrible duel, renewed every day. And the earth alone remains immortal, the mother from whom we arise and to whom we return [etc.]

> Qu'est-ce que notre malheur pèse, dans la grande mécanique des étoiles et du soleil? Il se moque bien de nous, le bon Dieu! Nous n'avons notre pain que par un duel terrible et de chaque jour. Et la terre seule demeure l'immortelle, la mère d'où nous sortons et où nous retournons [etc.]

This is not indirect speech, and at first sight it seems to be direct speech, with the first person and the present tense. However, it does not purport to give Jean's actual words or precise thoughts; the author has told us that it is the gist of Jean's confused reverie. And the 'we' that he uses does not relate to a specific group of people, it means here mankind as a whole. The impact of these reflections is indeed somewhat similar to that of free indirect speech. But, however we

121

define the form, how strange is this hymn to the earth in the mouth of a simple soul like Jean! He is abandoning the village in great discouragement, and could hardly find satisfaction in the thought that the vice and crimes he has witnessed and suffered from are somehow compensated by the constancy of the earth. We are here absorbing the rhetoric of the author, who is using Jean as his mouthpiece; the 'we' and the present tense are the forms the orator uses when addressing his audience. In this type of writing we can properly speak of a narratorial abuse.

VIII

Dostoyevsky and the flux of experience: *The Idiot*

There are several pitfalls attending the application of our analysis of free indirect speech to Russian. The meaning attached to some of the deictic particles like 'here' and 'tomorrow' may be nothing like so precise as in the western European languages, and may be misinterpreted when we read a translation. The sequence of tenses is much less rigid, and very often the tense of a statement in indirect speech does not accord with the governing, introductory verb; a statement like 'he went on thinking' will probably be followed by the present tense, 'what a disgusting pimple that fellow *is*'. I am not competent to say how far a native Russian-speaker feels such a present tense to imply presentness, but it is certainly inadvisable to make any rigid supposition. In cases like this, translators correctly use in English the past tense, 'was'.

In spite of these provisos, there can be no doubt that there is free indirect speech in Russian, as a distinctive stylistic form, identical in all its main features with that in the western European languages, except in respect to the sequence of tenses —and we must not forget what Bally noted, that French or English FIS enjoys great freedom in this respect. Also, these main features can be preserved in scrupulous translations, so that these may, with prudence, be used for our present purpose.

We find a number of isolated cases of free indirect speech in Turgyenev, from the early *A Sportsman's Sketches* (1852) to the late *Torrents of Spring*. But it is in no sense a characteristic feature of his style. It is also to be detected, just here and there, in Tolstoy (notably in *War and Peace,* in a few odd passages giving Nicholas Rostov's thoughts); but its absence is much more remarkable than its very slight presence. For that extraordinary classicity of Tolstoy's style, that epic clarity and firm serenity of vision, may be attributed in no small measure to the constant unity of the narrative perspective, the absence of those switches to the character's perspective that are denoted by free indirect speech. It is amazing that *War and Peace* (1865–8) appeared in the same decade as Dostoyevsky's *Crime and Punishment* (1865–6) and *The Idiot* (1869), for they seem to belong to different worlds, stylistically as well as in other ways. And with Dostoyevsky free indirect speech is not occasional, even if not frequent, but deeply characteristic. Though it shows some of the features we have observed in his European contemporaries, it also develops new functions, of the greatest importance for the later novel.

The theme of M. M. Bakhtin's brilliant study of Dostoyevsky is that the structure of all the novels is 'polyphonic', as opposed to the 'monological' form of the traditional novel.[45] While, in the latter, the narrator is the final authority as regards the truth and moral bearing of his story, Dr Bakhtin claims that in Dostoyevsky's novels the narrator's views, judgements, even knowledge, constitute only one contribution among many, and are often subordinate in significance and insight to those of the characters, especially of the 'heroes'. Thus the novels are never rounded off, given a definitive summing up, by the narrator; their deepest significance lies in the subjective experience and interpretation of the characters. Dr Bakhtin examines various aspects of the novels that substantiate his thesis, but in his remarks on the different forms of speech (narratorial report, direct speech, dialogue, monologue) he does not comment on the presence of free indirect speech. Yet this might have both supported his theory and at the same time led to some modification, as I hope to show.

No reader can fail to notice how, in Dostoyevsky's works, the events and the reactions of characters seem almost to escape the control of the author, overflow their own confines, lead away in previously unsuspected directions. In so loose a structure one might expect to find free indirect speech as the medium through which the thoughts of a character repeatedly assert themselves in their own idiom, breaking through the framework of narratorial description. And this, indeed, does occur. But FIS does not do so as frequently or systematically as in Flaubert or Trollope. Dostoyevsky still uses very fully the older methods of reproducing the inner motions of the mind—narratorial report, direct speech, and the soliloquy in inverted commas—as well as FIS. The latter usually occurs at times of great inward tension, struggle, and anxiety—in *Crime and Punishment*, for instance, when Raskolnikov arrives outside the old usurer's, just before he commits the murder, or when in part VI he is on his way to Svidrigailov's. Yet it does not occur in all situations of stress. When it does so, it usually signifies both tension and loneliness, and takes the form of soliloquy, inward argument and inward dialogue, rather than that of actual spoken dialogue.

The emotional stress that evokes FIS also tends to disrupt it, so that we often meet passages that mix various forms in a freer way than would be usual in English. Some of the complications are illustrated in the following passage from *Crime and Punishment* (part VI, chapter 3); the narrative proceeds in this way for several pages. I translate as literally as possible from the Russian:

> In all these days a certain thought went unremittingly through Raskolnikov's head, causing him great distress, although he even made efforts to drive it away—so burdensome was this thought. He sometimes thought: Svidrigailov was constantly circling round him and is still doing so; Svidrigailov has learned his secret; Svidrigailov has had [had had] some designs upon Dunya. And what if he still has them now? It can almost certainly be said that he does. And what if he, having learned his [Raskolnikov's] secret and thus having gained power over him, will now get the wish to use it as a weapon against Dunya?
>
> This thought would sometimes torment him even in a dream, yet this was the first time that this thought appeared before him so consciously and clearly, now, when he was on his way to Svidrigailov.

It will be seen that the reported speech of the second sentence starts like simple indirect speech, with only the conjunction 'that' missing; the past tense is used and the third person for the person of the thinker. But already in the last part of this sentence 'and is still doing so' we leap into the present tense, and the present reference is maintained in the forms 'has learned' or the future 'will', as well as the simple present, till the end of the paragraph. Yet these present-tense forms are combined with the third person. The form is halfway between direct speech ('Svidrigailov has learned my secret, he will now get the wish', etc.) and the normal indirect form, which is reestablished with its familiar features in the opening of the new paragraph. The effect of the present tense is to convey Raskolnikov's excitement and anxiety most urgently to us, by putting us at his temporal level, at the 'now' explicitly mentioned in the final line of the passage quoted. Such complexities of syntax reveal greater psychological complexities than does the normal free indirect speech that we have analysed in French, English and German writers; they seem to penetrate into more obscure psychological processes.[46] This, I believe, is the most striking characteristic of Dostoyevsky's use of free indirect speech. As his use is never simple, it is best if we make a fuller analysis of a single, longer passage.

This passage occurs at a high point in *The Idiot,* part II, chapter 5, and we can be content to use, by kind permission of Penguin Books Ltd, the reliable translation by David Magarshack.[47] After a series of exhausting encounters, which have excited him and involved him in the fates of numerous persons, Prince Myshkin returns to St Petersburg, takes a room at a hotel, and then wanders through the streets. He is acutely anxious for Nastasya Filippovna, who he knows is in danger from her uncontrollable lover Rogozhin, to whom he is attached with a strange feeling of brotherhood. Myshkin knows, too, that he himself is in danger from Rogozhin, who he suspects is trailing him, and he imagines that a knife he has seen on Rogozhin's table is the murder weapon. A newcomer in Russia after a long absence, his mind is much concerned with a series of brutal murders that have recently been committed in the capital. A thunderstorm is brewing, and to cap it all Myshkin feels that the strain of the last few days is bringing on an attack of epilepsy, the signs of which he knows well. Before our passage opens, there is a narratorial description of the visionary effect of these fits, the 'curious reality' that supersedes the normal, the 'intense heightening of awareness', the mysterious elimination of time, and this account prepares the reader for the strange confusions, the imposition of a subjective reality upon a reality that is recognisable and understandable, that distinguishes the whole section until the moment when the fit engulfs the Prince.

It is easier to follow if the passage is broken into smaller pieces:

> He was suddenly seized by an intense, irresistible desire, almost a temptation. He got up from his seat and walked straight out of the gardens towards the Petersburg suburb. A short time ago he had asked a passer-by on the Neva Embankment to point out to him the Petersburg suburb across the river.

The 'desire' is to find Nastasya Filippovna's house, though her name is not mentioned until, after much wandering, he arrives there, to be told that she has left the city. 'Ago' usually means a past measured from this present moment, and hence here seems to indicate that this last sentence is formed from the Prince's subjective perspective. But the Russian 'davecha' can mean either the subjective 'ago' or the objective 'before', so that the sentence might as well be narratorial as free indirect speech. It seems to be growing more common to use 'ago' in both senses in English, too.

> It was pointed out to him, but he had not gone there. Besides, it would have been useless to go there to-day: he knew that. He had long known the address; he could easily have found the house of Lebedev's relation, but he knew almost for certain that he would not find her at home. 'She has certainly gone to Pavlovsk or Kolya would have left a message at The Scales.' So if he was going there now, it was not, of course, because he hoped to see her. Another sombre and tormenting curiosity tempted him now. A new, sudden idea came into his head . . .

> But for him it was quite enough that he had set off and knew where he was going: a minute later he was again walking along without being aware of his surroundings. The thought of the implications of his 'sudden idea' became all at once repugnant to him and almost impossible. He gazed with painful strained attention at everything that caught his sight; he looked at the sky, the Neva. He spoke to a little child he met. Perhaps his epileptic condition was becoming more and more acute. The storm, he felt, was really coming nearer, though slowly. He could already hear the distant thunder. It was getting very close.

While the latter part of this passage is narratorial, there are several indicators in the first half that ensure that this formulates Myshkin's own thoughts and feelings. An inner argument is denoted by such particles as 'almost for certain', 'of course', 'perhaps', and 'to-day' places the reader in Myshkin's temporal situation. At one point a thought is put in inverted commas, but this does not mean that it is actual speech; this form simply serves to distinguish a clearer thought from the vaguer thoughts, intentions, apprehensions, that race through his mind.

Even here, it is not all FIS; the last two sentences of the first part might be narratorial, like much of the last (incidentally, 'without being aware of his surroundings' is not quite correct; 'without observing the way he was taking' is closer to the Russian, and does not suggest so advanced a paranoia). But throughout, the distance between the narratorial perspective and the subjective perspective is very slight; the narrator seems only to confirm what the character is more or less conscious of, and does not explain or clarify what is obscure to Myshkin. That who 'she' is, and what the 'sudden idea' is, are not explained is understandable within the statements in free indirect speech, since the Prince himself does not need to make explicit something of which he is aware and which he may, for various reasons, prefer to suppress. It is remarkable however that the narrator, in the narratorial sentences, also does not enlighten us, and this curious relationship of narrator and character seems to confirm Bakhtin's analysis.

> For some obscure reason he could not now get out of his head Lebedev's nephew [a nihilistic advocate of violence], whom he had seen that morning, just as sometimes one cannot get out of one's head some persistent and stupidly tiresome tune. The strange thing was that he kept thinking of him as the murderer whom Lebedev had mentioned when introducing him to the young man. Yes, he had read about the murderer not so long ago. He had read and heard a lot of such cases since his return to Russia; and he had followed them up carefully. And that afternoon he had been very interested in his talk with the waiter about that same murder of the Zhemarins. The waiter agreed with him, he remembered that.

We might read much of this as narratorial; the temporal indications almost invite us to do so, but actually, in the Russian, they ('that morning', 'that afternoon') can bear either a subjective or an objective reference. But if it is read as narratorial, then 'for some obscure reason' or 'the strange thing was' seem to be a rather arbitrary enhancement of mystery on the part of the author. If however it is read as free indirect speech, i.e. as Myshkin's own awareness, then such phrases are meaningful, the reason is obscure to *him,* and *he* feels it strange that he confuses Lebedev's nephew and the murderer. The exclamation 'Yes' strongly asserts it as FIS, and this is confirmed by 'he could not now get out of his head' at the beginning, and 'he remembered' at the end. It is very noticeable that, repeatedly, a phrase that at first seems vague, arbitrary, or even clumsy, reveals itself as psychologically significant once it is read as FIS. Thus the 'persistent and stupidly tiresome tune' would be an idle authorial remark, but is significant for Myshkin; that 'he followed them up carefully' interprets his own estimate of 'carefully'; the rather feeble 'very interested' is appropriate to his state of mind.

> He remembered the waiter, too; he was not at all a stupid fellow, reliable and careful, but 'still, goodness knows what sort of fellow he was. It is difficult to make out the new people one meets in a

new country'. He did, however, begin to believe passionately in the Russian soul. Oh, during those six months he had been through a great deal—a great deal that was new to him, a great deal that he had never suspected, nor heard, nor expected! But a stranger's soul is a dark mystery, and a Russian's soul is a dark mystery—a mystery to many.

As before, the inverted commas indicate thoughts that emerge in more tangible clarity out of the chaotic musings of the Prince. The exclamatory sentence beginning 'Oh' assures us that the whole passage is free indirect speech. As before, sentences and epithets which, if narratorial, would seem vague or clumsy, are precise and subtle when we understand them as the thought of the character; precise and subtle, that is, in delineating his thought and interpretation of experience.

In the Russian, some of the temporal indications make the subjective references clearer than they are in the translation. 'He did begin' in Russian is an imperfective, and would be more accurately translated 'He was beginning', and this latter form, like the French 'imparfait', suggests reported speech. 'During those six months' should be, more correctly, 'during these six months', referring us to Myshkin as the temporal point of reference.

In Russian, present-tense forms of the verb 'to be' are often omitted from an affirmative sentence, and this is so even when such sentences are part of indirect speech. Other verbs too, though belonging to indirect speech, may appear in the present tense, when in English (and French and German) the past would be required. It is noticeable that the translator of *The Idiot* usually replaces these present tenses by the past, since this is more natural in English. In the continuation of our passage there are so many examples of this change that I put in square brackets the present tense that is, in some cases, actually used by Dostoyevsky, and in others is 'understood' in the absence of a verb.

He had been friends with Rogozhin for a long time, they had been intimate friends, they had been 'like brothers'—but did [does] he know Rogozhin? But what chaos, confusion and ugliness there sometimes was [is] in all this! And what a disgusting and conceited pimple that nephew of Lebedev's was [is]! 'But what am I saying?' the prince went on thinking to himself. 'Did he kill those creatures, those six people? I seem to have got it all mixed up—how strange it is! My head seems to be going round and round. . . . And what a dear, what a charming face

Lebedev's daughter has—the girl standing up with the baby—what an innocent, what an almost childlike expression and what an almost childlike laugh!' It was [is] funny how he had almost forgotten that face and only remembered it just now. Lebedev, who stamped his feet at them, probably adored [adores] them all. But what was [is] truer still, what was [is] as certain as that twice two makes four, was [is] that Lebedev adored [adores] his nephew too!

I believe that if the passage is read with these present tenses in mind, our direct experience of the mental processes in the Prince is enhanced. All the same, Mr Magarshack was quite right to turn them into the past tense, and thus to affirm clearly the nature of the passage as free indirect speech. That he was aware of the problem is clear from a change he has made. There are in the Russian text no inverted commas for the Prince's ruminations that are given in the first person: 'But what am I saying? Did he kill etc.'; they are not distinguished typographically from the preceding and following free indirect speech. But Mr Magarshack has perceived that, since he uses the third person and past tense for the FIS, he should distinguish through inverted commas these sentences in the first person and present tense, just as Dostoyevsky sometimes uses inverted commas to distinguish more articulate thoughts from the vaguer. Quite consistently, the translator uses the phrase 'But what am I saying', when the Russian has 'What am I up to?'. In spite of these differences between the Russian and English texts, which are imposed by the difference between linguistic habits, the main features of free indirect speech are easily recognisable in Russian, though the narrator is here most unobtrusive, and detectable mainly through the syntax.

The next paragraph opens with further exclamatory questions and further particles indicating an inner argument ('certainly', 'still'):

Still, why should he pass so final a judgement upon them, he who had only appeared that day? Why should he pronounce such verdicts? Lebedev had certainly set him a problem that day: had he expected a Lebedev like that? Had he known such a Lebedev before? Lebedev and Du Barry—good heavens! Still, if Rogozhin did kill, he would not kill in such a horrible way.

This is emphatic FIS, yet the Russian text evokes the character-perspective still more strongly than the translation, for 'that day' is literally 'today', and 'if Rogozhin did kill' is 'if Rogozhin were to kill'.[48]

Free indirect speech remains prominent throughout the whole of chapter 5 of part II, ceasing only with Rogozhin's attempt on the life of Prince Myshkin, which is foiled by the onset of the latter's epileptic fit. At this point the narratorial voice takes over, to describe the fit and the steps taken to bring the Prince into the care of friends.

The most remarkable feature of Dostoyevsky's use of free indirect speech is something that goes beyond what we find in earlier writers. It arises from his grasp of the peculiar nature of that self-communing that we have examined in *The Idiot,* when a character, committed to a purpose felt to be obligatory but unsure about facts, about judgements, and about tasks, is wrestling with unmastered experience. We see how his thoughts ramble, how accidental their sequence is; important insights jostle with insignificant, purposeful understanding is crossed by thoughts and generalisations that do not clarify and are to no purpose; the Prince is borne along in his search by something not quite translatable into rational terms, sometimes by meeting objects that exert a powerful attraction yet whose associations are unclear and resist formulation into words. All these various thoughts, memories, impressions, intentions, encounters are not logically structured, yet they are by no means accidental; random in incidence, none is superfluous. Not only do they echo and illuminate what has been happening to the Prince and around him, but they themselves seem to want to order themselves in a meaningful pattern, to shape themselves into some decision. One is tempted to say that the eddies and wisps of thoughts in his head are a sort of review presided over by his unconscious will rather than by his conscious reason; but this would be incomplete. For his conscious will, conscious intentions, his rationality are all in play too, puzzling, checking, searching, combining. What can confidently be said is that all the functions of the psyche are active together, and all contribute to the attainment of some deeper understanding and consonant action.

As the supreme medium for this self-communing, Dostoyevsky chooses free indirect speech, especially for situations of high tension. He uses direct speech, of course, in many situations. But direct speech cannot go much beyond those thoughts that are ripe for verbal expression, and in situations where they are communicable to others. Direct speech is also used for certain types or parts of soliloquy, yet it remains hampered by the element of conscious verbalisation that is inherently in it. On the other hand, simple indirect speech is very rarely used, since it not only fails to reproduce the vigour and vivacity of a character's responses, but also ascribes to the reporting narrator a sovereign control and understanding that conflicts with the adventure of exploration that is being played out before us. Free indirect speech extends here beyond the reproduction of actual speech or formulated thought, it is used to convey, as well, all that mass of impressions, associations, memories, and impulses that accompany and underlie thought and resolve. We can, indeed, no longer divide the novel, as we can with Jane Austen and Goethe, into two different modes, narrative and speech (direct or indirect). Here, the narrative itself may be conducted in free indirect speech, and nowhere more clearly than in the chapter we have been examining. That is, the events as they occur, the Prince's wanderings through St Petersburg, the pursuit by Rogozhin, the visit to Nastasya Filippovna's and the return to the hotel are experienced by us through the experience, the consciousness of the Prince. We do not only share his thoughts, we know the events almost solely through him.

A curious aspect of this procedure emerges, that we meet frequently in and since Joyce's *Ulysses*. The gain in authenticity and directness of experience is accompanied by a loss of clarity. There is a striking instance of this in this same chapter 5. We learn that the Prince has been fascinated by an article in a shop window and that, becoming aware of this and wondering what it was that fascinated him, he finds his way back to the shop to see what it was. It is an article costing 60 kopeks, and the price makes him laugh (p. 257 in Magarshack's translation). But we do not get an inkling of what the article is till page 265, when the Prince remembers having caught a glimpse of Rogozhin watching him as he paused in front of this article 'with a hartshorn handle', and only on the following page does he explicitly link it up with the knife he had earlier seen on Rogozhin's table. We experience what the object means for the Prince only as he does, with his suppressions, his confusions; our clarification occurs step by step with his. So, likewise, we are no more sure than he is that Rogozhin's eyes are tracking him throughout his wanderings, until we and he see Rogozhin waiting on the dark stair with uplifted arm.

This chapter seems to bear out Bakhtin's thesis of the 'polyphonic' novel, in which the narrator has no more authority than the characters and can attain no higher viewpoint, 'optique', than that of his hero; an art in which there is no higher truth than the experience of the hero can convey and in which this experience is not subject to an objective appraisal and correction. It is indeed remarkable that one of the most distinctive features of FIS throughout the century, the implicit or explicit irony in the narratorial tone, is quite absent here, in relation to the hero. The narrator is implicitly present in the indirect form, but his role excludes both irony and avowed sympathy, and is confined to that of an instrument of communication between the hero and us, the readers. But if in some of Dostoyevsky's modern successors we do find a relativism and subjectivism of the type Bakhtin defined, the latter's thesis does not do full justice either to *The Idiot* as a whole or his work as a whole. The events of this chapter itself are prefaced by a narratorial explanation of the experience of an epileptic fit and of the strange 'reality' the victim experiences, and it is in the first stages of such a state, immensely enhanced by agitation, bewilderment, and anxiety, that the events take place and are narrated in the way analysed. In no other way than through the experience of the Prince could these particular events be understood. Dostoyevsky therefore seems to justify the extended use of FIS in this chapter on grounds that would not apply in other parts of his narrative. In his other novels Dostoyevsky also uses extended free indirect speech only on certain occasions, when the intensity of feeling in his characters justifies a temporary obliteration of a more generally recognisable objective reality.

Now, it is true that in the major novels there is no significant role allotted to the narrator; as Bakhtin says, he cannot find words that would sum up the meaning of the novel. But I believe the narrator plays a more important part than Bakhtin allows. Even in this chapter 5, the narrator sets the scene and closes the incident. The story as a whole is his product, only he can connect and relate these many characters and incidents, can reduce them to a story, and thus present them to us as a complex but comprehensible whole. It is only he who provides the point from which all that occurs is retrospective, the point, that is, which makes a tale tellable.

It is true that the narrator of *The Idiot* does not provide explicit explanations and interpretations; indeed in chapter 9 of the last part, the narrator, using the editorial 'we', writes:

> We find it extremely difficult to continue without certain explanations. Yet we feel that we have to confine ourselves to a bare statement of facts, if possible, without any special explanations, and for a very simple reason: because we ourselves find it difficult in many instances to explain what took place.

But such modesty is a little suspect. The narrator may well claim that many sorts of human behaviour cannot be 'explained', and that, in particular, the Prince cannot be understood on normal rational or scientific grounds. But the arrangement of his story, the manner of its ending, even if they do not yield explicit evaluations, show clearly enough where spiritual significance lies and offer the reader the chance of imaginative experiences that lead to the same conclusion. The modesty of Dostoyevsky's fictive narrator, in *The Brothers Karamazov* as well as *The Idiot,* does not disguise that 'sagacity' of the good writer that Nietzsche recommended: 'It is very well-behaved and very sagacious to leave your reader himself to utter the last quintessence of our wisdom.' In any case, the postulate of the narrator, however retiring he may be, is in itself a guarantee that there is a point outside the characters and events from which the experiences related can be ordered and valued. The stylistic device of free indirect speech, which so intimately fuses narrator and character, seems so characteristic of the nineteenth century since, while allowing a large space to the subjective view, it still does not shatter the objective framework.

IX

Conclusions

The texts discussed in this book illustrate various functions of free indirect speech as it occurs in the nineteenth-century novel, and I believe the roughly historical arrangement corresponds to the progressive discovery of the resources of this stylistic form. It does not claim to be a history of its invention and use, for its origins go much further back and, also, it is used on many occasions by many other nineteenth-century authors. All that can be claimed is that authors and works have been chosen in which either its use is significantly bound up with the whole character of the work or in which its relatively slight use gives a clue to its functioning.

Thus, the absence of many authors from our texts does not mean that FIS is not to be found in their works. It may, for instance, be thought that since no German texts apart from Goethe and Büchner are included, there is no FIS in German narrative fiction between them and Thomas Mann's *Buddenbrooks,* to which incidental reference is made in Part I. This conclusion would be quite wrong. Herdin's remarkable dissertion of 1905 was devoted to the German novel, and was the first study to comment on the incidence of this stylistic form in a number of authors between Wieland in the eighteenth century and Fontane, Herdin's (older) contemporary. Herdin's list has been much enlarged since, and it would now include such writers as E. T. A. Hoffmann, Mörike, Droste-Hülshoff, Otto Ludwig, Spielhagen, Arno Holz, and Clara Viebig. But in none of these authors, except perhaps the Holz of *Papa Hamlet,* is free indirect speech more than an occasional adventure, in none does it represent a whole narrative stance. *Papa Hamlet* might have deserved inclusion here, if only because the presence of FIS in this piece of Naturalist prose has so consistently been overlooked; but there is nothing unique about Holz's use of FIS, and in any case I have already discussed it elsewhere.[49] And free indirect speech in *Buddenbrooks* has been the subject of studies by Lerch and Hoffmeister, to which I need add nothing.

On p. 21 above I listed some questions that the early controversy over the newly identified form had left unanswered. I believe that the analysis of texts has allowed us to investigate them, with one large

135

exception. I am not referring to the limitation of these investigations to prose. For, while the verse epic and the ballad might well have been included, I do not think they would have thrown additional light on the nature of the phenomenon examined, and would certainly have required a consideration of other problems that would have made this book more unwieldy than I wished it to be. The big omission is non-fictional prose, history or biography or even literary criticism. In his original articles Bally included these in his scope and offered illustrations of 'le style indirect libre' from such works.

It is not difficult to find instances of this style in historical and literary studies; I myself have occasionally used it in this book, when reporting the opinions of scholars. As a means of reproducing someone else's argument it is a pleasant variant from direct quotation, which is often too long or awkward to fit in, and from simple reported speech, which can easily grow clumsy and wearisome. It allows one to give the actual words and tone of the writer, and to fit them smoothly into one's exposition. It offers too a seductive opportunity, often alluded to in the course of our textual analyses, for a 'narratorial' distortion that insinuates a loaded comment, of irony perhaps, into what is ostensibly a faithful reproduction. But much the most important use is in history or biography, where, in addition to the reporting of the actual spoken or written words of a historical character, the author may also be inclined to report the thoughts, the mental processes, of a person in the vivacious form of free indirect speech. It seems to me to be here a very dangerous form, even if it rests on actual authentic documents; for it both evokes very precisely the formulations in the head of the person, and also easily conveys a subliminal authorial suggestion. Above all, free indirect speech postulates a relationship between narrator and character, a knowledge of the inner processes of another person, that can never exist in real life, and that inevitably introduces a fictional element if it is used in historical writing. When once discussing the use in historiography of the tense called the 'historic present', I defended its lack of favour among historians with the argument: 'Dramatic effects they need not fear where the occasion is dramatic; but fictional effects they must dread.'[50] I think historians feel the same reluctance about the use of free indirect speech, and are well advised to prefer either the actual words of their historical characters or a narrative form that clearly demarcates the sphere of the narrator from that of the character.

The results of the present investigation can be briefly summed up thus. Free indirect speech is a stylistic device based upon the form of simple indirect (reported) speech, i.e. using the tenses and person proper to the latter. It injects into this rather colourless form the vivacity of direct speech, evoking the personal tone, the gesture, and often the idiom of the speaker or thinker reported. In its simplest form it is found in the mimicry of odd expressions characteristic of a person, but in more complex, extensive forms is used for the dialogue and the articulate soliloquy, short or long, as also for pre-verbal levels of nervous and mental responses, and non-verbal registrations of sense-impressions, ranging from the most evident and readily expressed observations to the most obscure movements in the psyche. While certain of these functions are found in first-person novels, the most remarkable have evolved in association with the undefined, non-personal, third-person narrator. Its great fulfilments are associated too with point-of-view narrative, i.e. the narrative form in which the non-personal narrator aligns himself intermittently with various characters, or constantly with the 'hero', and describes through their eyes. It has thus meant a great enrichment of narrative style, since its use permits us to see the fictional characters moving not merely against the background of the narrator's consciousness, but within their own worlds of perception and understanding.

However, this is not all. It has been an important result of the textual analyses, that this style does not, in the nineteenth century, mean a radical subjectivisation of the fictional world. Critics have indeed often maintained that the use of free indirect speech permits the reader to experience fully and exclusively in terms of, and from the perspective of, the character, the subject. But this is not the case. Mimicry itself, as Leo Spitzer wrote, implies a mimic as well as a person mimicked; and the effect (and the fun) of mimicry depends on our awareness of the difference between the imitation and the real thing, as well as the likeness. That is, the narrator is always effectively present in free indirect speech, even if only through the syntax of the passage, the shape and relationship of sentences, and the structure and design of a story; usually, of course, he also appears as the objective describer of external events and scenes and of psychological processes, and as a moral commentator. Above all, perhaps, as the agency that brings multiple and complex events into relationship with one another and leads them to an end that establishes, even if without explicit comment, an all-embracing meaning.

It is usual to consider the further development of free indirect speech in this century, in the work of James Joyce, Virginia Woolf, William Faulkner and others, to be a consequent release of the subjectivism inherent in this form. Thus, when J. W. Beach (*The Twentieth Century Novel*, 1932) or J. Pouillon (*Temps et Roman*, 1946) speak of the disappearance of the narrator in the modern novel ('exit author'), they mean that the narrator submerges himself in his characters, and that the reader lives with the characters in the immediacy and indeterminacy of the present, shares their experience, but being deprived of a narrator's independent voice lacks an authoritative, objective, standard of truth or morality. As Pouillon puts it, the classical novel always establishes a 'general psychological value, distinct from and superior to the values of the characters; but in Faulkner, Dos Passos, and such moderns, there is no such general value. The reader can participate in the experience of the characters, he cannot judge or know. With this diminution of the narrator's function, 'story' itself begins to disappear, becomes discontinuous, fragmentary, full of accident, since it is essentially the narrator who creates the retrospective perspective from which happenings can be woven into a coherent story.

Though there clearly is, in the works of that modern generation of which these critics speak, a marked tendency towards subjectivism of this kind, I do not believe their generalisations are fully valid. Wolfgang Kayser rightly detected in the over-all design, the subterranean connections, of Joyce's or Virginia Woolf's novels evidence of a controlling narrator;[51] and I would add that the free indirect speech that is still, with them, a prominent feature, always bears the signature of the narrator. Its abundance in Solzhenitsyn's novels demonstrates that FIS does not necessarily imply the undermining of narrative or ethical objectivity. At the same time, the ease with which, in Joyce's *Ulysses*, FIS merges into direct speech, involving changes in tense and person, indicates the more fragile hold of the narrator, as compared with his sovereignty in the classic free indirect speech as used, for instance, by Flaubert.

A more fundamental attack on the classical tradition of the novel is delivered by a later generation, for whom Joyce and company also belong to the past, and it is in their creative work and criticism that a more searching criticism of free indirect speech is implied. One of the first signs of this criticism is to be found in Musil's view that story, the retrospective connection of events and people in a causal sequence, with a definable outcome, is a fiction imposed on a chaotic world by human beings who only in this way can escape from bewilderment and despair.[52] Imaginative fiction, therefore, threatens to become not a reflection of reality but a deception, an illusion, an escape. This type of criticism may be applied to all types of coherent statements, as in

Auden's sonnet, 'Words':

> A sentence uttered makes a world appear
> Where all things happen as it says they do.

Such criticism of the structure and presuppositions of the traditional novel became a most vigorous challenge in the work of Sartre, for instance his novel *La Nausée* and his treatise *Qu'est-ce que la littérature?*, in which he sought a type of narrative that would capture 'the uncertainties and risks' of life in the present, and escape the deceptive and 'deathly' coherence created by the retrospective narrative with its foregone conclusions.[53] Roland Barthes' *Le Degré zéro de l'écriture* (1953) pungently sums up this radical repudiation of the traditional novel. He attacks the structural postulates of connection, order, and development, whether attributed to events or to personal psychology, that underlie both historiography and the novel. The coherence these assert in history, the patterns they establish in personal relations and the relations between individuals and the social world, are in Barthes' view only myths that falsify reality; if one says, in the famous phrase of Camus, that a novel turns a life into a destiny, one is not justifying art but destroying its credentials of authenticity. Similarly, the third-person novel, the postulate of a narrator who can know the inner workings of the characters and draw numerous characters and incidents into a meaningful relationship with a meaningful outcome, is held to be a profoundly deceptive falsification of human existence. This hidden, omniscient narrator is the aesthetic counterpart of a now discredited providential God, who for each believer turns the world into *his* world, a universe there for his purposes and centred upon his welfare. Even the normal narrative tense, the preterite, is for Barthes a falsification, suggesting definiteness and completion in events that are necessarily incomplete and ambiguous.

For Barthes, these falsifications are not fortuitous, but the means by which the bourgeois class has asserted its self-confidence and created the psychological conditions for its power and survival. With this large assumption we cannot concern ourselves here, though it would seem that the artistic conventions against which Barthes is rebelling extend far beyond any specifically bourgeois period and art, and are presuppositions of civilisation altogether, rather than of a particular class or age. What is relevant here is the conclusion concerning narrative form that Barthes draws from his unremitting emphasis on authenticity. For while he prefers among the traditional forms the first-person novel, he most warmly recommends what he calls the 'neutral' narrator, the toneless reporter of facts, without foreknowledge, retrospective knowledge, or insight, writing in a style that confines itself to establishing the barest relationships between characters and resists all the seductions of evocative and expressive description.

These tenets correspond to a modern trend that we might chiefly associate with Sartre, Camus, and Robbe-Grillet (even though the reduction of the narrator's role in the latter's *Le Voyeur* paradoxically turns the whole novel into explicit and implicit free indirect speech). In this modern trend, the narrator's experience does not transcend that of the 'hero' (who may himself be the narrator), who has no more or deeper, often indeed less, knowledge than other characters, since he has no access to their secret thoughts or their memory. If events occur, the narrator is as ignorant or bewildered as any participant or bystander; if any explicit meaning emerges, it is only such as an observer might infer, and as ambiguous. There are many variants of this type, some of which in their search for authenticity, renounce identifiable characters and coherence of narrative and narrative perspective, like Robbe-Grillet's *La Jalousie*.

This modern trend impinges directly upon the theme of this study, since in this type free indirect speech is an inner contradiction. The demise of the authoritative third-person narrator in effect spells its doom, since FIS prospers only in his atmosphere. The power, implicit in free indirect speech, of penetrating the innermost psyche of characters and of reproducing their mental processes in narrative form, constitutes in Barthes' view one of the great superstitions, since it fortifies us in the belief that the world may be understood and ordered in terms of a personal destiny. So, in fact, free indirect speech is to be found scarcely at all in the work of many leading and innovatory writers, though it may survive, not only in more conventional writers but also in those who, like Saul Bellow, powerfully continue a tradition.

The question this modern trend makes us ask is serious and important: Is free indirect speech essentially a historical form, a symptom of a historical phase that is now, perhaps, growing obsolete? One hesitates with an answer, partly because one is sceptical of self-proclaimed modernisms. Throughout all the modernism of the 1920s, 1930s, and 1940s, a Thomas Mann could not only cling to, but powerfully re-assert the role of the story-teller. Today, Günter Grass or Solzhenitsyn are towering exceptions to the rule. But, fortunately, we are not required to answer the question in this form. What we can confidently say, and what the study of free indirect speech can demonstrate, is that this stylistic form, so rich in its achievement, can indeed be inappropriate to certain types of narrative, irrelevant or hostile to their vision and purposes, and hence in certain periods meaningless and functionless. If we are now in such a period, it is all the more desirable that we should be able to discern free indirect speech in the contexts in which it has exerted an important function, and to understand something both of its technical structure and its artistic and psychological implications.

Notes

1. The critical prefaces have been collected, together with an introduction by R. P. Blackmur, in *Henry James: The Art of the Novel*, 1935.
2. Käte Friedemann, *Die Rolle des Erzählers in der Epik*, Berlin, 1910 (reprint Darmstadt, 1965).
3. Oskar Walzel, 'Objektive Erzählung', *Germanisch–Romanische Monatsschrift (GRM)*, VII, 1915–19, reprinted with amendments in *Das Wortkunstwerk*, 1926.
4. F. K. Stanzel, *Die typischen Erzählsituationen im Roman*, 1955.
5. A. Tobler, 'Eigentümliche Mischung direkter und indirekter Rede' and T. Kalepky, 'Verschleierte Rede', both in *Zeitschrift für romanische Philologie*, XXI and XXIII, 1897 and 1899. E. Herdin, *Studien über Bericht und indirekte Rede im modernen Deutsch*, diss. Uppsala, 1905. C. Bally, 'Le style indirect libre en français moderne', *GRM*, IV, 1912, pp. 549–56 and 597–606. This was followed by a second article, 'Figures de pensée et formes linguistiques' in the same periodical, *GRM* VI, 1914, pp. 405–22 and 456–70.
6. T. Kalepky, 'Zum Style indirect libre (Verschleierte Rede)', *GRM*, V, 1913.
7. E. Lorck, 'Passé défini, imparfait, passé indéfini', *GRM*, VI, 1914, particularly pp. 181–3.
8. E. Lerch, 'Die stilistische Bedeutung des Imperfektums der Rede (style indirect libre)', *GRM*, VI, 1914, pp. 470–89. This excellent essay seems to have been overlooked by Germanists, perhaps because its title does not suggest a connection with German literature. Thus Werner Hoffmeister, who prefaces his substantial study of 'erlebte Rede' in *Buddenbrooks* with an account of Bally's 'style indirect libre' and the controversy it aroused, and who includes this essay of Lerch's in his bibliography, shows no awareness of the fact that Lerch's article is a valuable anticipation of his own study.
9. Lerch, *loc. cit.*, p. 482. Lerch contrasts *Buddenbrooks* with *Die Wahlverwandtschaften*, which has an obtrusive narrator; the

choice was unfortunate, since Goethe's novel is full of free indirect speech.

10. *GRM,* VI, 1914.

11. *Ibid.,* p. 417. It is not clear why Bally states that this procedure of Zola's is 'just the opposite' of what Kalepky means by 'verschleierte Rede'; but he had reason to be irritated by Kalepky's niggling criticism.

12. A. Thibaudet, *Gustave Flaubert,* second ed., 1935, pp. 230–2. This section of Thibaudet's study was taken over from the first edition of 1922 without substantial alteration.

13. L. Spitzer, 'Zur Entstehung der sog. "Erlebten Rede" ' and E. Lerch, 'Ursprung und Bedeutung der sog. "Erlebten Rede" ', both *GRM,* XVI, 1928.

14. Oskar Walzel, *Gehalt und Gestalt im Kunstwerk des Dichters,* 1924, pp. 380–2; and *Das Wortkunstwerk,* 1926, pp. 207–30.

15. The distance between normal usage and free indirect speech becomes so great at times as to seem too audacious a challenge. Thus the form of Walter Scott's 'necessity had no law', quoted above (p. 49), though grammatically correct, sounds odd and may mislead—like the piece of reported speech from *Buddenbrooks* that Lerch discusses: 'Sie hatte, strafe sie Gott, niemals eine schönere Braut gesehen' (the equivalent of 'She had, so help her God, never seen a lovelier bride'), where the exclamatory oath sounds slightly absurd when put into the third person.

16. Marguerite Lips, *Le Style indirect libre,* 1926. In the Grammatical Notes appended to vol. I of R. W. Chapman's edition of Jane Austen's novels, there is no indication of the form that Bally had defined and Marguerite Lips discovered in *Sense and Sensibility.*

17. Käte Hamburger, *Die Logik der Dichtung,* 1957. See my résumé of Dr Hamburger's thesis and the controversy raised by her book ('Tense and novel', *The Modern Language Review,* LVII, 1962). To my criticism of Dr Hamburger's denial that the preterite of fictional narrative has a temporal significance I would add, with W. Hoffmeister (*Studien zur erlebten Rede bei Thomas Mann und Robert Musil,* 1965, pp. 26–7), that she was misled through failing to recognise the subjective nature of the tense of verbs in free indirect speech.

Dr Hamburger's discussion of the temporal deictic particles remains most valuable. She rightly observes that they much more decisively establish the temporal situation of the fictional character than do the spatial particles. 'Here', 'there', 'to the right', etc. are often used without a subjective reference. There is in modern writing a great loosening of the meaning of temporal adverbs too. 'Now' has for a long time meant 'at that moment' as well as 'at this moment'; 'ago' is frequently used to indicate 'before that time' as well as 'before the moment where I now stand'. In some writers even 'tomorrow' and 'yesterday' are used in the sense of 'the day after' and 'the day before'. This lack of discrimination is regrettable, since it means a loss and can produce a misunderstanding. A similar trend is evident in German, for instance with 'morgen' and 'gestern'.

18. S. Ullmann, *Style in the French Novel*, 1957, and N. Page, *Speech in the English Novel*, 1973.

19. Walzel wrote an account of 'erlebte Rede' in 1924 for *Zeitschrift für Bücherfreunde*, NF, 16, and, abbreviated, for his book *Gehalt und Gestalt im Kunstwerk des Dichters*, 1924. The fuller version was reprinted in *Das Wortkunstwerk*, 1926. The titles of articles by Lorck, Lerch, and Spitzer here quoted, and of Hoffmeister's book, are given in Notes 7, 8, 13, and 17 above.

20. A useful analysis of the different forms of inner monologue is to be found in Derek Bickerton's 'Modes of interior monologue', *Modern Language Quarterly* (Seattle), 28, 1967.

21. Dorrit Cohn, 'Narrated monologue. Definition of a fictional style', *Comparative Literature* (Oregon), XVIII, 1966; L. W. Kahn, 'Erlebte Rede in Goethe, *Die Wahlverwandtschaften*', *PMLA*, March 1974. Dorrit Cohn's useful account contains a full bibliography of the theoretical discussions of 'style indirect libre' and 'erlebte Rede', including the few studies available in English and those on the occurrence of the style in English literature.

22. See Kahn's study, quoted in Note 21, though Kahn sees only the ironical function of FIS in this novel. Although Walzel mentioned in his accounts of 1924 and 1926 that 'erlebte Rede' is used in *Die Wahlverwandtschaften*, scholars still ignore its presence. Kahn notes with some indignation the recent comment of a distinguished scholar that this novel holds no trace of 'the psychological perspective of a character' (R. Brinkmann, *Wirklichkeit und Illusion*, second ed., 1960), and he points out an evident error in interpretation in H. G. Barnes's *Goethe's Die Wahlverwandtschaften*, 1967, a misreading of a passage of FIS as a straightforward objective authorial statement.

23. Page references are to the convenient Reclam edition of *Die*

Wahlverwandtschaften. The novel has been reliably translated by H. M. Waidson under the title *Kindred by Choice* (1960).

24. There are many examples of this type of irony: Eduard—I, 2, 12; I, 18, 141; II, 13, 266; Charlotte—I, 11, 101 and 102; I, 13, 111; I, 13, 126; Ottilie—II, 9, 232; the Gehülfe—II, 17, 212, etc. A charming example occurs when, in a conversation between Eduard and the mondaine Baronesse, Ottilie is referred to, in ostensible narratorial form, first as 'the dear child' and then as 'that insignificant newcomer of a girl' (I, 10, 95).

25. Graham Hough has admirably defined the character and function of this impersonal narrator in *Emma*, particularly those features of the narratorial style (in Hough's terminology 'authorial' or 'objective' narrative) that establish the authoritative status of such statements in respect to truth and morality ('Narration and dialogue in Jane Austen', *The Critical Quarterly*, XII, 1970).

26. *Sense and Sensibility, The Novels of Jane Austen*, ed. R. W. Chapman, vol. I, chapter 1, p. 5. All page references are to this edition.

27. *Sense and Sensibility*, chapter 2, p. 8.

28. See pp. 83, 96, and 101.

The extraordinary freedoms enjoyed by modern writers in this respect can be inferred from the following passage from Saul Bellow's *The Victim* (1947), a novel in which the narrative is conducted predominantly in free indirect speech, interrupted by conversations and snatches of soliloquy in direct speech. It will be observed how easily the past tense of the indirect speech is replaced by the present tense, and vice versa (pp. 88–9, Weidenfeld and Nicolson edition of 1965):

'There was something in people against sleep and dullness [. . .], Leventhal thought. We were all the time taking care of ourselves, laying up, storing up, watching out on this side and on that side, and at the same time running, running desperately, running as if in an egg race with the egg in a spoon. And sometimes we were fed up with the egg, sick of it, and at such a time would rather sign on with the devil and what they called the powers of darkness than run with the spoon, watching the egg, fearing for the egg. Man is weak and breakable, has to have just the right amounts of everything—water, air, food; can't eat twigs and stones; has to keep his bones from breaking, and his fat from melting. This and that. Hoards sugar and potatoes, hides money in his mattress, spares his feelings whenever he can, and takes pains and precautions. That, you might say, was for the sake of the egg. Dying is spoiling, then? Addling? And the last judgment, candling? Leventhal chuckled and rubbed his cheek. There was also the opposite, playing catch with the egg, threatening the egg.'

29. Confusions can occur in indirect speech in ordinary conversation as well as in imaginative literature. The other day I came into our sitting-room and, surprised not to find my wife there, called out to her 'Fania'. She answered from upstairs, and called down: 'What is it?' I answered: 'Oh, nothing, I was only wondering where you were'—and immediately corrected myself and said 'where you are'. In fact, my grammar had been perfect, but it held an ambiguity, for the past tense of reported speech, though determined by the introductory verb and itself temporally colourless, does easily acquire a temporal implication of its own.

Similarly, the impossibility of finding a satisfactory indirect form for exclamations which imply a first or second person, like 'Just think' or 'Bless me' or 'My God', is often felt as an irritating obstruction. In a recent novel by Margaret Forster, *Mr. Bone's Retreat* (Secker and Warburg, 1971), a passage of FIS communicating Mr Bone's reflections on what a visitor had said to him contains the following: 'Sophie *had* said many nice things. She had told him how she used to walk across the Park [. . .] and how she had always wanted to live in Jonquil House—oh, excuse her, it was no longer called that, was it?' (p. 38). 'Excuse her' is either a naive attempt to find the correct indirect form for 'excuse me' or more likely a bit of stylistic fun by the witty author. Such exclamations are variously resistant to transference into the third person, and in close contiguity we find in Thomas Mann's *The Magic Mountain* 'Gott mochte ihm helfen' ('Might God help him' as the indirect form of 'May God help me') and 'Sie hätten ihr ein wenig Sonnenschein gebracht, mein Gott, wohl den letzten', where 'my God' is indirect speech. Of course, a particular narrative context or personal style will also decide choices of this kind (Thomas Mann, *Der Zauberberg*, 1924, vol. I, 'Walpurgisnacht', pp. 505 and 509).

30. *Mansfield Park* forms the third volume of the Chapman edition.
31. Graham Hough, *loc. cit.*
32. I have used the text of the Inselverlag edition, George Büchner, *Werke und Briefe*, n.d. There is a good translation by Michael Hamburger in G. Büchner, *Lenz and Woyzeck*, University of Chicago Press.

33. Büchner, *Werke und Briefe,* pp. 83–4, 87, 88, 89.
34. Page references are to the New Illustrated Dickens, *Bleak House,* 1951.
35. Lisa Glaser, *Die Erlebte Rede im englischen Roman des 19 Jahrhunderts,* Bern, 1948.
36. *The Mill on the Floss* is referred to by the abbreviation *MF;* page references are to the Everyman edition, reprint 1972. It will be noticed that, in this piece of FIS, Mrs Glegg once refers to herself not as 'she', as in normal indirect speech, but as 'her sister Glegg'. The replacement of the first-person pronoun by the third is the normal rule for direct speech, but sometimes the elimination of the first (and of course second) person may cause confusion, especially when the third-person pronoun is used for both the subject of the FIS and other persons. In such cases writers often use the name of the person speaking or thinking in place of the pronoun.

The same device is used in the German reported speech with the subjective, and shows the close relationship between free indirect speech and normal indirect speech. In Siegfried Lenz's *Das Vorbild,* 1973, where this form of reported speech is repeatedly used, we find the speaker/thinker whose words are being reported is typically referred to as 'Er, Pundt, übersehe nicht ...', 'Ihr, Doktor Rita Süsseldt, könne . . .'. Occasionally the specific designation of 'he' or 'she' is used both for the speaker and a person spoken of or to (see p. 102). The slightly pedantic effect is deliberately evoked by Herr Lenz.
37. Since the chapters of *Middlemarch* are numbered successively, there is no need to refer to the 'books' into which the novel is divided. The abbreviation *MM* is used, and page references are to the Penguin edition, reprint 1972.
38. Page references are to the Everyman edition of *Barchester Towers,* reprint 1945.
39. The World's Classics edition of *Is He Popenjoy?* has been used. The quotations from chapter 32 will be found in vol. I, pp. 313–15.
40. All quotations and page references are from the edition of *Madame Bovary* in *Œuvres Complètes de Flaubert,* 1902. There is a reliable translation in the Penguin Classics (1975) by Alan Russell.

I owe the reference to the stylistic argument at the *Madame Bovary* trial to H. R. Jauss, *Literaturgeschichte als Provokation,* 1970, pp. 203–6.

41. Hugo Friedrich, *Drei Klassiker des französischen Romans,* 2nd ed., 1950, pp. 151–4.
42. References to Zola will be found in M. Lips, *op. cit.,* pp. 50 and 70. Bally speaks of Zola's 'abuse' of 'style indirect libre' in 'Figures de pensée', *GRM,* VI, 1914, p. 417.
43. E. Zola, *Germinal,* Paris, 1885. References are to this edition. There is a reliable translation in the Penguin Classics (1958) by L. W. Tancock.
44. E. Zola, *La Terre,* 1887, p. 103. References are to the edition in Bibliothèque Charpentier. The translation in the New English Library, under the title *Earth,* is severely abridged and of no use for our purposes here.
45. M. M. Bakhtin's *Problems of the Work of Dostoyevsky* appeared first, in Russian, in 1929, then, in a revised edition, in 1963, with the title *Problems of the Poetics of Dostoyevsky.* This appeared in French translation as *Problèmes de la poétique de Dostoïevski,* trans. G. Verret, Lausanne, 1970. An English translation appeared in 1973, but I have used the French version. It is to M. M. Bakhtin's brother, Nicholas Bakhtin, formerly Reader in Linguistics in the University of Birmingham, that I owe my introduction to modern linguistics, and it has been a constant source of regret to me that, owing to his death in 1950, I have not been able to discuss this present study with him.
46. In *Ulysses,* the soliloquies of Stephen and Bloom often switch from the normal indirect form (third person and past tense) to the first person and present tense. The increased immediacy due to this change is to be felt, but it does not perform the function to be discerned in Dostoyevsky's syntax.
47. Dostoyevsky, *The Idiot,* trans. D. Magarshack, Penguin Classics, 1971, part 2, chapter 5, pp. 260–9.
48. The Russian tenses offer insuperable difficulties to the translator, whose rendering must inevitably be insufficient, perhaps even misleading to some extent. Among other difficulties, the pluperfect in English ('had had', 'had been seen') has no exact parallel in Russian, its purpose being served by the past tense of the perfective aspect of the verb, which however in some contexts may best be rendered by a normal past definitive. The choice between these two may be a stylistic choice between reading a passage as free indirect speech or as objective narrative. For instance, part 8 of *Anna Karenina* in Aylmer Maude's translation (World's Classics ed., vol. II, p. 382) opens: 'Nearly two months had gone by. It was

already the middle of hot summer, but Koznyshev was only now preparing to leave Moscow.' This reads much like FIS, our time-perspective being aligned with Koznyshev's. But the more correct translation would start 'Nearly two months went by', and this sounds like normal narratorial report, in which the impact of the following 'now' is changed and comes to mean, as often, something equivalent to the objective 'then' rather than the subjective 'today'.

49. 'The prose-style of naturalism' in *Erfahrung und Überlieferung, Festschrift for C. P. Magill,* ed. Robinson and Siefken, 1974.

Dr J. A. Reddick has drawn my attention to the incidence of FIS, among other narrative forms, in E. T. A. Hoffmann's *Der goldene Topf* (1814), and only after some hesitation did I decide not to include an analysis of this Novelle in my text. There are two main reasons for not doing so. First: Hoffmann's story is built upon the polarity between sober, practical reality and a coexistent spiritual reality. The latter appears primarily through insights and fantasies of the hero Anselmus, and often takes the form of free indirect speech. The fundamental purpose of the Novelle is to present what are ostensibly the 'delusions' of Anselmus as intimations of a deeper spiritual existence, i.e. to claim that what is ostensibly subjective is in truth objectively real. This daring and skilful use of FIS contradicts its most essential function, as we discover it in the nineteenth century, to give a subjective statement the force of an objective one, without depriving it of its subjective status. For all its brilliance, Hoffmann's use is an eccentric one.

My second reason is Hoffmann's recurring use of a personalised narrator, who addresses the reader direct and frequently expresses his personal opinions, often with exclamations like 'alas!', 'in short', 'yes!' ('ach!', 'kurz', 'ja!') that may at other times function as indices of FIS. I have discussed, in relation to Thackeray and Trollope, the uncertainties of interpretation that arise, but they are more troubling in Hoffmann, since his personal narrator also drops into the role of the folk tale-teller, who readily accepts the reality of the irrational and magical events and hence confirms the objective truth of the subjective FIS.

Thus, while there are in *Der goldene Topf* cases of normal FIS, its functioning generally is untypical, and contains too many peculiarities to justify it taking a prominent place among the texts discussed in this volume.

50. R. Pascal, 'Tense and novel', *The Modern Language Review,* LVII, 1962.

51. W. Kayser, *Entstehung und Krise des modernen Romans,* 1955.

52. Robert Musil, *Der Mann ohne Eigenschaften,* 1952, p. 664: 'It occurred to Ulrich that the law of life for which, overburdened and dreaming of simplicity, one longs, is nothing other than the law of narration!—that simple order that consists of one's being able to say "When that happened, the other occurred!". It is the simple series, the reduction of the overwhelming multiplicity of life to one dimension, as the mathematicians would say, that comforts us; the stringing of everything that has happened in space and time on one thread, that famous "thread of the story", out of which the thread of life is made. Lucky the man who can say "when", "before" and "after" [...]. As soon as he is in a position to reproduce events in the sequence of their temporal occurrence, he feels so good, as if the sun were shining on his stomach.'

53. The most striking passages are to be found in *Qu'est-ce que la littérature,* 4, 'La situation de l'écrivain en 1947'. J.-P. Sartre, *Situations,* 2, 1948.